ORGANIZING EXTRA-CLASS ACTIVITIES IN PRIMARY CLASSES

Jumanyozova Mukhabbat
Olimboyeva Malohat

© Taemeer Publications LLC
Organizing Extra-class activities in Primary Classes
by: Jumanyozova Mukhabbat / Olimboyeva Malohat
Edition: August '2023
Publisher:
Taemeer Publications LLC (Michigan, USA / Hyderabad, India)

ISBN 978-93-5872-145-4

© Taemeer Publications

Book	:	Organizing Extra-class activities in Primary Classes
Author	:	Jumanyozova Mukhabbat / Olimboyeva Malohat
Publisher	:	Taemeer Publications
Year	:	'2023
Pages	:	96
Title Design	:	*Taemeer Web Design*

TASHKENT
2023

This methodical manual describes the ways of organizing and effectively conducting extracurricular activities in primary education, in particular, spiritual and educational activities. It contains scenarios of celebrations and events held in different directions.

The methodical guide is intended for primary school teachers and students studying in this field, and for all those who are interested.

Developers:
Muhabbat Jumanyozova – f.f.n., Assoc.
Malohat Olimboyeva - student

Reviewers:
Nukuljon Karimova is a teacher of the 5th general education primary class in the city of Khiva, Khorezm region.
Sanobar Ollaberganova - associate professor of the Department of Primary Education Methodology of UrSU, f.f.n

BEGINNING OF THE WORD

In the current era of globalization, effective forms and methods of preparing the young generation, who are our future, for life are being widely introduced based on the latest achievements of science and culture. Therefore, the development of high moral qualities in the society, formation of national ideology, education of young people in the spirit of respect for our rich cultural heritage, historical traditions, universal human values, love for the Motherland, loyalty to the ideals of independence is the decisive factor of all the reforms implemented in our country.

Primary education, as the main link of continuous education, occupies an important place in the education of the young generation. Educational work outside the classroom is also important in raising young people in a spiritually mature human spirit.

Development and implementation of effective organizational, pedagogical forms and tools based on the rich national, spiritual and historical traditions, customs and universal values of the people in the spiritual and moral upbringing of the young generation, organization of spiritual and educational work is manifested by doing. In this place, it is possible to emphasize the importance of spiritual and educational activities held in primary education, festive nights dedicated to various historical dates. Therefore, in this methodical manual, we considered it permissible to divide the spiritual and educational activities held in primary classes into three groups:

1. Events related to historical dates and holidays that have an important place in the glorious history of the Republic of Uzbekistan.

2. Events dedicated to the dates of birth of great scientists who have a special place in the history and literature

of the Uzbek people.

3. Events on various topics related to mother nature, community life.

The scenarios of holidays and events mentioned above were collected from the work experience of elementary school teachers working in general education schools of Khorezm region, from public publications, in particular, from "Primary Education" magazines.

SCENARIOS OF EVENTS ON HISTORICAL DATES AND HOLIDAYS WHICH ARE IMPORTANT IN THE GLORIOUS HISTORY OF THE REPUBLIC OF UZBEKISTAN

SEPTEMBER 2 - KNOWLEDGE DAY

"HELLO , SCHOOL"

The stage was festively decorated on the basis of the slogan BAYRAM in connection with the Independence Day of the Republic of Uzbekistan.

Leader 1: I am happy with you, sometimes I am
It was the day you cried, my dear.
My sweet tongue, I sound grassy,
You are my soul, my soul, Motherland!

Leader 2 : You are boston, my beautiful boston desert too,
My life without you, my way without you
Even my lake dries up without you
You are my soul, my soul, Motherland!
  Jambuling by the fountain is beautiful,
  A nightingale in love with a flower is beautiful.
  Your sons are beautiful souls.
  Your past is great, my great country!

1st presenter : - Assalomu-alaykum, dear teachers, dear guests, dear parents who send their dear children to the school, and students who strive for knowledge! Welcome to our night.

2nd presenter : - Hello, happy young people, youngers of my independent country, dear compatriots and contemporaries living in the free land, welcome to our party!

1st leader : - Today we are gathered here on the occasion of " Knowledge Day " , we will give the floor to the director of our school__ to open this event. *(Words of greeting)*

2nd presenter: - Even now, the celebration continues in our country. The 25th anniversary of our independence was widely celebrated yesterday. Every year, on the eve of Independence Day and " Knowledge Day ", dozens of newly built schools are handed over to students. Little hearts full of joy will enjoy the warmth of the newly built schools. Also, 1st graders who go to school every year are awarded with a special gift from the honorable President. It is a shining example of caring for the nation's children.

The attention of our country's president to small children always makes you " excellent " urges them to study for grades, to grow up to be a perfect generation and to take a place among the worthy children of this dear Motherland in the future.

1st presenter: - After the independence of Uzbekistan, serious attention is paid to the education of the young generation. Happy 31st day of freedom ! May the 31st moment of hurlik be blessed! May peace always create beautiful scenes of prosperity in our country! *(The national anthem of the Republic of Uzbekistan is performed and the national flag is raised).*

Speaker 2: As the poet said,
> To measure the value of every moment
> Scales of gold, less stones than diamonds.

The chairman of the Parents' Committee participates in our circle. Now let's give the speech to this dear guest. (*Words of congratulations*)

Leader 1 : The beginning of life begins with a song
> No one can live without a song.
> Even the sky and the sun listen to music.
> Nightingale also listens to the song for a while.

(*Girls perform a dance called "Uzbekistan Gulzor".*)

Starter 1: This is a beautiful boston that has no equal.
Gulistan from epics.
It is called Uzbekistan.

People love him.
Host 2: When wandering the valleys.
I had a strange feeling.
A garden that bloomed with a blow.
I would kiss the soil of the Motherland!
Now let's listen to the words of our teacher, labor veteran ____. *(Words of greeting)*

Leader 1 : - Thank you.
Istiklal, I die for you
Prayers and wishes are on my tongue day and night.
The joy of freedom is the path to happiness,
I am famous in the world, my beloved country.
(Students recite poems about the Motherland).
Leader 1: Bring back spring, bring back autumn, bring back cranes.
When he returned, the world was filled with joy.
Unknowingly, we get white hair.
When we remember our youth, the heart calms down.

Now the word it's the turn of our teachers to work veteran ___
(Teacher's congratulatory words).
Leader 2: The light of mercy always shines from your face, teachers.
I want to walk in your footsteps, teachers.
(Students perform the song "Dear teachers").
1st leader : Our independent country, our nation is our Motherland.
Love of the country, love of the heart is manifested in the heart.
Mother Uzbekistan is one and the same.
The world welcomes your great independence!
In the early mornings, holding a pencil,
Eighteen thousand worlds bloomed in my heart.

Motherland - said, my tongue wandered like a nightingale.

The Buharis even bowed down to you,

O teacher - first of all, Mr. teacher!

Leader 2: - Little brother who is stepping on the threshold of the school for the first time, protect your blessed book, protect your school, protect your class! Protect your dear school! Don't infect any of them! Listen to the teachings of the teachers. Remember the knowledge your teachers give!

Now the director of our school ceremoniously distributes the President's gift given by our head of state to the 1st grade students.

1st starter: - Graduate class student and 1st class students calls the students to class by ringing the first bell. *(The bell rings.)*

Starter 2: - Dear participants of the holiday, to conclude our event, the word goes to ___. *(Congratulations and Closing Remarks)*

OCTOBER 1 - DAY OF TEACHERS

"WE BOW TO YOU, TEACHER"

(The event begins with the singing of the national anthem of the Republic of Uzbekistan.)

Leader 1: Hello dear people,
　　　　　　The heart of the sun.
　　　　　　From the light of your mercy
　　　　　　Happy young people.
　　　　　　From the heart for you
　　　　　　We say the word.
　　　　　　We bow and say,
Everyone:　Hello, hello
Leader 2: My teacher is my first teacher,
　　　　　　You are dear like a mother.
　　　　　　He shined a light on our path
　　　　　　Without the sun on earth.
　　　　　　Giving knowledge to life
　　　　　　You are the one who sent it.
　　　　　　You have been very kind,
　　　　　　We bow to you.

All: Be happy a long year

1st presenter: - Dear teacher. Today is your holiday. May this day be blessed. We wish you health, long life, patience, happiness and luck.

an easy task to teach a child a letter , therefore, in all times, the holders of this profession were honored and respected by the people.

Since 1997, October 1 - "Teachers and Mentors" Day" has been celebrated as a national holiday in our country. This is the great respect of our government and our President for teachers and trainers, the high appreciation of their work.

To reveal this event, the word is given to__. *(Words of greeting)*

Leader 2: Are words enough to describe?
　　　　　　Dear teacher.

His mind is wise, his mind is deep,
Jonahon teacher!

1- starter: Hold a pencil in my hand,
Give a book first.
Was there a wayfaring star?
Dear teacher!

Leader 2: Your words are wise
Enlighten our hearts.
light our way
Dear teacher!

(Song "Teachers" will be performed by students)

Leader 1: Who taught you a letter on the path of truth with pain,
It's not easy to sell it, it's worth a thousand dollars.

Leader 2: - You are right, we owe a lifetime to the teachers who gave us knowledge, taught us to read and write, and taught us the science of life.

1- presenter: - Among the people there are sayings: "A teacher is as great as your father", "A scholar who learns by asking what he does not know is a tyrant who does not ask." If we ask the teacher what we don't know, he will teach us everything he knows. Now the students of our class will recite their memorized poems to their teachers.

Student 1: When he first steps into school
love from you teacher .
To write and read husnikhat
Master, I learned from you!

Student 2: My mind has changed completely
you taught letters.
heart ,
I learned to read from you.

Student 3: You taught me kindness,
Show service to the people.
You have done a lot of this kind of advice,
I learned to live from you.

4th student: Cultivating manners in the heart,
You read a whole book.
heart now,
I learned everything from you.
(*A song about teachers is performed.*)

1- Leader: - Now the students recite a poem dedicated to their teacher.

To the first teacher: First, moving slowly to the desk,
Holding a pencil in my little hand,
I never sleep
A teacher like you!

To the school principal: Your kindness is a lively river,
Your heart is an endless river.
You are kind and gentle,
Head to everyone at school.

To the teacher of "Etiquette":
We kept asking questions,
What is right, what is fair?
decency in our hearts,
You shine like the sun.
O loving teacher,
Obeisance to you, glory to you!

To the teacher of "Russian language":
You taught Russian
Here is my letter.
C pasibo vam dorogaya,
Oil uchitelnitsa rodnaya.

1st presenter: - Dear guests, let's present our flowers to the teachers. (*Teachers are given flowers*).

2- presenter: - Now, let's turn to the notebook, what kind of person is the teacher?

Student 1: Master, everything is clear to him
Student 2: The teacher gives knowledge from the heart.
Student 3: The teacher also has a teacher.

Student 4: The teaching profession is responsible, hard, but very honorable.

Student 5: The teacher is the leader of the world of knowledge.

Student 6: The first teacher is a person who imparts knowledge to the mind, spirituality to the heart, and spreads knowledge.

(Students dance to the Khorezm song "Diga-digajon")

1- presenter : - In order to become a teacher, to develop the intelligence of others, to enjoy the benefits of enlightenment, to educate as a real person, the educator himself must meet these requirements!

Leader 2: - We are proud to mention _____ who has received such a great name.

(Songs are performed by students.)

1st presenter : - Dear teachers, now watch the songs prepared for you. Laugh, you will live long.

(Scenes about the lives of students and teachers will be shown)

Leader 1: - Dear teachers! Our event prepared for today's holiday has come to an end.

Leader 2: - However, our love, loyalty, and respect for you will never end.

(Dance "Khorazm Lazgisi")

"RESPECT TO THE TEACHER"

(The stage will be festively decorated. Films from the "First Call" event and lesson processes will be shown on the monitor based on the song about teachers.)

Leader 1: A beacon in the ocean of life,
Look at the distance, teachers.
Giving lessons to loyal students,
Teachers are always on the right path.

Leader 2: With composure in the most difficult moments,
They will learn the lesson of perseverance with patience.
Instill goodness into hearts always,
They bear sweet fruit for the future.

1st presenter: Hello guests, dear intellectuals,
Their faces are the sun and their hearts are rivers
Respect to you, peers,
With our hands on our chests, we say hello!

Leader 2: Hello, master teacher,
The architect of education, the jeweler of the dice,
Your holy profession is a seal for the ages
The real gem of life...

1st presenter: - Hello, selfless, passionate, patient, full of goodness, enlightening teachers and coaches and guests of our event!

2nd presenter: - Today, we have given our hearts, eyes, and love for the future of the Motherland, taking upon ourselves the responsible and honorable task of raising a well-rounded, well-rounded generation for the great Uzbekistan. We have gathered to congratulate and honor our teachers, teachers and coaches who have decided to do their work seriously.

1st presenter: - Master, teacher, teacher, coach. Although these words do not exactly repeat each other, they are close in meaning. In essence, the universe is the embodiment of meaning. First of all, the person who taught how to write and read is a teacher.

2nd presenter: - This is the teacher who instilled love for books after learning to read and write! This is our first teacher, who is happy if we study well, if we know less than excellent, he immediately puts his hand on our heart and directs us towards knowledge!

Leader 1: - In fact, our people, who see the fulfillment of all their dreams and happiness in the maturity of their children, have always glorified the breed of teachers and showed them infinite respect and will continue to do so.

Honor the teacher from time immemorial, my people,
I have the right to wish them well.
You are so great, so clever,
Your life is a miracle - my mind is not enough.

Leader 2: - Indeed, the contribution of teachers in fulfilling the huge, laborious and noble task of teaching students by accepting them as their own children, showing love and giving knowledge is huge. Teachers and mentors who dedicate their lives to enlighten the path of others can be compared to a torch.

1st presenter: - Dear teachers, we will give the turn to the students whom you have brought up and are teaching science and craft.

Student 1: Is there anyone who has not received your education?
It was the first light in your hearts.
A scientist, a poet or an artist,
For the first time, he looked up to you as a teacher.

Student 2: In the pain of a single letter,
The result is a person who has gone out of the blue.
No wonder you are happy,
This is the moment when he stands up and bows.

Student 3: An example of grace like Alisher the Great,
How painfully did you teach literacy.
Is it possible to pay off this debt?
Can it be broken with a hundred gems?!
(Students demonstrate their dance).

1st leader: - The word teacher evokes feelings of deep respect and boundless gratitude in the heart of every person.
For you, coach man,
For every knowledge.
For us without a leader
The heart is a river, teachers.

2nd presenter: - In the saying of our people: "If you want to worry about life in a year, plant wheat." If you worry about life ten years from now, plant a tree. If you want to worry about the life after a hundred years, give education.
We kept asking questions,
What is right and what is honest?
decency in our hearts,
You shine like the sun.
Oh, kind, dear teacher,
Obeisance to you, glory to you.

Leader 1: - Dear teachers, there are questions hidden in the balloons in front of you, please choose the ones you want and answer the questions (the following questions are hidden in the balloons).

1. Who was your first teacher?
2. Why did you choose this profession?
3. What profession did you want to have when you were young?
4. Tell me the most memorable and interesting story from your school days.
5. If you could find a magic candle, if you only had one wish to ask, what would it be?

(The song "Dear teachers" is performed.)

2nd presenter: - Dear teachers, we sincerely congratulate you once again on your happy day.

1st presenter: - We wish you good health and success in your difficult and honorable work of raising the young generation.

Leader 2: - May you all be blessed to see the growth of

your students and children. This is the end of today's celebration. Thank you for your attention!
(Dance performed by the teacher and students).

OCTOBER 21- THE DAY WHEN THE UZBEK LANGUAGE WAS GRANTED THE STATUS OF THE STATE LANGUAGE

"MOTHER LANGUAGE IS THE SUN OF MY HEART"

1 - leader: My mother tongue, you are the highest mountain in greatness,
My mother tongue, you are the Erami garden in my love.

2 - presenter: Mother tongue, soul tongue,
In my heart
My singing nightingale.

1 - presenter: - Hello, dear teachers, dear students.

2- presenter: - Hello, participants and guests of our round.

1st presenter: - Today is a big celebration in our country, that is, October 21 - the day when the Uzbek language was granted the status of the State language of the Republic of Uzbekistan.

Leader 2: - In this regard, the students have prepared an event called "My mother tongue is the sun of my heart". Please listen and watch.

1st presenter: - Many countries in the world have their own national language. The Republic of Uzbekistan also has its own state language. This is written in Article 4 of the Constitution of the Republic of Uzbekistan, the main law of our republic: "The State language of the Republic of Uzbekistan is the Uzbek language."

Head 2: - The state language means the language that is the main means of communication in the territory of this state. All state documents are written in the state language. Meetings are conducted in this language.

Leader 1: - Each country ensures the purity of its language, its enrichment and tries to expand the range of consumption, creates favorable conditions for learning and teaching the national language.

2nd presenter: - The Law of the Republic of Uzbekistan on the State Language was adopted on October 21, 1989. Therefore, our people celebrate this day as a language holiday every year.

Leader 1: - On this day, we will sing poems and songs about our mother tongue. Remembering the rich and long history of our language, we remember the memory of writers, poets, scientists who contributed to its development.

2nd presenter: - Our classmates will read Khurshid Davron's poem "Mother Tongue".

Student 1: How many worlds have passed away,
Life laughed, death cried.
Grandfathers died because of you,
They left, you stayed my tongue.
2nd student: Koshgari on your swing
He sang the old song
And to your rustling leaves
Navoi gave his blood.
Student 3: When Babur was leaving Samarkand,
Suffocate the sorrow in the heart,
He took away from his motherland,
My Turkish language is only you.
4th student: Mashrabmas, you hanged on the gallows,
Nadiramas, you are slaughtered.
Don't worry, my tongue
Your head is broken, your eyes are carved.
Student 5: But the hero killed by the enemy
Resurrected again for revenge,
Forever you are and forever able
Sound the ground to fill.
6th student: He sacrificed his life for the country,
Cross the fire, enter the river,
All the blood your children shed
You shuddered like a weed.
Student 7: My mother tongue, live forever,

I won't die even if you're gone
If I'm speechless, I'm like you, Oybek
I ask with my eyes.

2nd presenter: - Thank you, we will give the turn again to poems praising our mother tongue.

" My mother tongue will not die" *(Erkin Vahidov's poem).*

" My mother tongue" *(Mirtemir's poem).*

" Language" *(Avaz O'tar's poem).*

Leader 1: - Why do we need the law on the state language ? said Hero of Uzbekistan Erkin Vahidov.

Student 1: - There are as many languages as there are nations, peoples, peoples on earth. There is no nation without a language, and there is no language without a nation. These are twin concepts. They cannot be separated from each other. If subtracted, both lose their identity. A nation merges with another nation.

Student 2: - Every nation uses mainly one language as a tool of communication throughout its life.

3rd student: - Mother's role in raising a child and bringing it to adulthood is incomparable. It is called mother tongue because the child hears and learns the first sounds and words from his mother.

Leader 2: - The national language is the first sign of the nation. Therefore, when every nation fights for a future, it first fights to restore the purity of the national language and its dignity. Language is also a bridge that conveys the results of experience and knowledge of past generations to future generations. Language makes a person know himself, perfects the sense of national pride.

Leader 1: - The following narrative is a clear example of this.

(The narration called " The Power of Language" is staged and performed).

In ancient times, there was a leper daughter of a wise and

righteous man. Two guys fell in love with this girl. The girl did not know which of them to like. The guys are running around trying to catch up with the girl. Finally, the girl said to them: " I want to be a mother to a son who can become a child of the country ." I need to know how you can raise him. I will tell you my decision based on that."

- This work can only be done by me. I will teach him science. I teach mathematics and calamity. Engaged in politics. Learns foreign languages. He will spread the world, - said the first guy.

When it was the turn of the second, he said: " The main wealth passed down from generation to generation is language. The length of a nation's life is determined by its language. All the beauty in the world and the happiness of listening to the magical mother alla is in the lap of the tongue, maybe you understand my purpose? I will teach my son not to betray his language, to tell songs, fairy tales, epics, and not to spare his life for our mother tongue."

The scholar laughed at these words and accused his opponent of being weak-minded. " Don't quarrel," said the girl, "there is a great sage in the country, we will go to him." Everything will be solved there. His judgment will be the law for me."

They went to the sage. He listened to all the arguments that caused the conflict and said to the young man who was accused of being mentally retarded: "I don't know if the girl loves you or not, but you deserve the honor of fatherhood...".

2nd presenter: - Our people, there is an Uzbek child who is not indifferent to our mother tongue, who today remembers our great grandfather Mir Alisher Navoi with pride and respect. No one has done more for the development of the Uzbek language and literature than Alisher Navoichalik.

Our grandfather discovered the beauty of the unique treasures of our beautiful language and used them in his works so skillfully that his popularity spread throughout the East. As the Sultan of Poetry said:

The throne of Olibmen is easy for me to decree,
Khitodin to Khurasan, without any hesitation.

Reader: It is a saying that a target gives life to the dead.
It is a word that gives a message to the soul.
Man is a very animal.
You know, there is no gem more precious than you.

Speaker 1: - One of the famous writers compared the unused word to a nail stuck in a green tree. In fact, a word used inappropriately, whether in oral communication or in the press, is considered a disregard for language in addition to the impression of melting.

2nd presenter: - "The father of the word is the mind, the mother is the language," - old people say. In the culture of communication, the word takes power from the mind and discretion from the language. A person's manners are first seen in his language, and then in his knowledge through his language.

Leader 1: - The scene that we want to show proves once again what language is capable of.

(The narrative below is dramatized).

One day, the king said to his ministers: "Cook me the most delicious food." The ministers consulted and cooked a dish of tongue meat. The food pleased the king.

He ordered: - Now bring me food prepared from the most bitter thing. This time they also cooked him tongue meat. The execution of the commission was acceptable to the king and he rewarded his ministers.

2 - presenter: - It's time for proverbs and poems about the culture of speaking.

(Students say proverbs and poems one by one).

1 - presenter: - Alisher Navoi, after discovering the treasures of his mother tongue, described it as follows: " Our language is such a treasure that is bigger than 18,000 worlds, and every word is a gem, that is, words are more than the lights of the sky." bright, such a flower is more beautiful than tulips.

Dear children, you are the owners of this great treasure. Keep it and cherish it.

2 - presenter: - It is our duty to follow the manners of communication in conversation, to express opinions depending on the situation, to treat people with consideration of age, to speak beautifully and meaningfully - this is one of the signs of humanity.

Leaders together: - Goodbye. Bless you!

DECEMBER 8 – CONSTITUTION DAY OF THE REPUBLIC OF UZBEKISTAN

"OUR CONSTITUTION IS OUR HAPPINESS"

An enlarged copy of the Constitution hangs in the center of the stage, which is festively decorated with flowers. Representatives of law enforcement agencies and guests are invited. The anthem of the Republic of Uzbekistan is played.

Speaker 1: How delicious the word motherland is,
You are worthy of everything dear.
Respect each and every boy and girl,
Holy, honorable great, my country,
Even if I die, I will not leave your arms.

Leader 2: The joy of the homelands is a masterpiece,
You are alone in the world.
A butterfly on your brow for a lifetime,
My country, I will say that it suits you.

2nd presenter: - Dear teachers, dear scholars and dear guests. Welcome to the holiday event dedicated to the day of adoption of the Constitution of the Republic of Uzbekistan.

1st leader: - Now we invite our guests, lawyers, to our circle. *(Let the lawyers speak)*

2nd host: Why I love Uzbekistan
The soil turns into a cup.
How to call the earth and sky the homeland
I call you holy, you call me secluded.

1st student: - We are citizens of Uzbekistan, as we admit this, our hearts are filled with pride and joy. Because Uzbekistan is a beautiful and unique country that has no comparison in the world.

2nd student: - To be born in such a country, to grow up enjoying its blessings, to be a worthy successor to the great people who delighted the world is a great happiness, an incomparable happiness that not everyone gets.

Student 3: - The legal basis of the citizenship of Uzbekistan is defined in the Constitution of our country, the civil code and other legal documents.

Student 4: - The word "citizen" means citizen. "Citizen" is a Latin word that means belonging legally to a country.

Student 5: - In ancient times, instead of the word "citizen", words such as "class", "raiyat" were more used in the sense that a person feels his rights and duties as a human being and his responsibility to the state and society. used.

6- student: - Being a citizen of Uzbekistan not only gives us pride, but also gives us a great responsibility. Because today's development of our country, future destiny, strengthening its place and influence in the world is our sacred duty, citizens of Uzbekistan.

7th student: - The sense of citizenship is very important in the formation of the virtue of patriotism. A person who deeply feels his civic duty respects the laws of the country and strictly follows them, he feels the will of his people in every clause of the laws.

Student 8: - Living with a sense of citizenship always requires conscious and active action, combining personal interests with the interests of the country and people. A person who feels a sense of citizenship connects the fate of his neighborhood, city-village, country with his own fate. According to the words of the first President, he will always "burn for my people and my country".

Student 9: - A conscious citizen is a citizen who thinks deeply and thoughtfully participates in events in the life of the society, who looks after not only his own interest or the interest of the group or category to which he belongs, but also the interest of the people and the homeland.

10th student: - Cultivating the will consists in directing feelings and desires to a specific goal, overcoming fleeting desires and inclinations, training the soul and body. For this, it is necessary to constantly practice, study a lot, not to be afraid of difficulties, to overcome them with patience.

11th student : - As our poet Gafur Ghulam said,
"A great son of a great country,

Know that the country is waiting for you."

12th student: - The nation refers to all citizens of one or another country. People - the leading power of the state are the people living in the society.

Student 13: - The people are the only source of state power. State power in the Republic of Uzbekistan is exercised only by the authorities authorized by the Constitution of the Republic of Uzbekistan and the laws adopted on the basis of the interests of the people. (Constitution of the Republic of Uzbekistan, Article 7.)

Student 14: There is no one like this beautiful boston,
A flower that has grown in epics.
It is called "Uzbekistan".
People love him.

Student 15: - According to the Constitution of the Republic of Uzbekistan, a citizen of the Republic of Uzbekistan who is not younger than 35 years old and has lived in the territory of Uzbekistan for at least ten years can be elected to the position of President of the Republic.

16th student:-- The President of the Republic of Uzbekistan is the head of state and ensures the coordinated operation and cooperation of state authorities. (Article 89)

17th student: Patriotic President, pride of my nation
He will think about his children tomorrow.
There is a sun in science
Tulips are basking in the light.

18 - student:- We always bow our heads in front of the bright memory of our respected and respected First President IA Karimov. We will not forget his advice to the youth, and we will justify his trust in us. All of us will certainly fulfill our filial duties and tasks before our Motherland and People with excellent grades and achievements in various fields.

Everyone: Mother Uzbekistan - our future,
It is our duty to study well.
Leader 1: Independence is a prospect
It means bright life.

The fortress is intact, the country is peaceful
Homeland means prosperity.
Leader 2: I will grow up, that's the intention
Let it be my wish.
Worthy of prospect
I wish to have a child.
(Students take turns reciting Qambar's poem "Bakht kamusi" and Dilshod Rajab's "Our main dictionary book").

1st host: - Since this is the year of "Dialogue with the people, human interests", the creative works carried out in our country are primarily for the people, for human interests.

Student 1 : - Every child has the right to have his own name, nationality, and the right to know his parents and their guardianship. (From the Convention on the Rights of the Child, Article 7).

Student 2: To our school garden
We spent a young sprout.
We took care of it
Do not let the sprout see.

Student 3: We are like a sprout
We are growing freely, happily.
The pride is with us
Motherland for life.

Student 4: Of our father and mother
We are the eyes that see
Mother Uzbekistan
The future is ourselves.

Student 5: - Our rights are fully specified in the Constitution of the Republic of Uzbekistan. Everyone has the right to ensure the safety of themselves and their children. He has the right to live in a safe environment.

Student 6: - We all have the right to live a good life. We have the right to have clothes, notebooks, pens and all the necessary things for a good life and rest.

Student 7:-- The right to life is the inherent right of

every human being. Attempting to kill a person is the most serious crime. (Article 24).

Student 8: - We have the right to be treated for diseases. Everyone has the right to use qualified medical services. (Article 40)

Student 9: - Each of us has the right to rest. Otherwise, we will not be able to find the strength to fulfill our duties.

10th student:-- Children have the right to education (i.e. study in school). Everyone has the right to education. (Article 41)

11th student: - Rights, in turn, remind us of our duties, studying for excellent grades is the main duty of every student.

12th student: - It is our duty to protect the environment, mother nature, birds and animals. Citizens are obliged to take care of the environment. (Article 50)

Student 13 :- Behaviors that are harmful to society and prohibited by law are called violations of rights.

ACTIVITIES OF THE STAGE

1. Aziza dances with the volume of the tape recorder turned up and disturbs the peace of the neighbors. Neighbors warn a couple of times.

2. Sardar calls his lieutenant Saeed once or twice in a loud voice. When Said did not answer, he threw a stone at his window and broke it.

3. Elbek draws pictures on the classroom desk and on the school wall.

Leader 2: - Yes, dear readers, while knowing our rights, we must also respect the rights of others, otherwise, we may face violations and sad events like the above.

Leader 1: - We all know that there are mandatory rules and laws established by our state and that the main task of these laws is to protect citizens.

Leader 2: - Because we truly love our homeland and are proud of it. And our love for our country is a sign of patriotism.

We, every citizen of Uzbekistan, are responsible for the prosperity and bright future of our motherland.

1- presenter: - As the first President stated, we are obliged to continue the great intentions and works of our great grandfathers.

2nd presenter: - That's why today's event has come to an end. Goodbye!

JANUARY 14 - THE DAY OF DEFENDERS OF THE MOTHERLAND

"DEFENSE OF THE MOTHERLAND - A SACRED CORNER"

The classroom is festively decorated, students bring the flag of the Republic of Uzbekistan to the sound of music. The anthem of the Republic of Uzbekistan will be played.

1st presenter: - Hello, teachers, dear guests.
Heart suns gathered in a circle.
I bow to you from the heart, respect from the heart,
Greetings, friends gathered for the holiday.

2nd presenter: - Hello, dear teachers, dear guests, dear students.

1st presenter: - Today, in connection with the Day of Defenders of the Fatherland, we will attend our event dedicated to the 30th anniversary of the establishment of our Armed Forces...

Together: -- Welcome.

1st presenter: - September 1, 1991. An age-old dream - hopes have come true. The independence of the Republic of Uzbekistan was achieved. In the form of an independent state, it got its own language, flag, coat of arms and anthem.

Leader 2: -- Our nation has committed itself to great work in order to build a free and prosperous Motherland, a free and prosperous life.

Student 1: Thank you, I have a world like you.
I have a loving wife like my mother.
I sing you and live for you
As long as I have blood in my heart and soul in my body.
O my conscience, my undying faith,
Thank you, my Uzbekistan.

2nd student: - Homeland is a holy place. Every inch of it is dear to us. There is a person who was born in this country, grew up and matured in this country, and lives with great love for it throughout his life.

3rd student: "Flowers are the garden of a peaceful country," our wise men say. We are thankful that our homeland is peaceful and our country is prosperous. Due to peace, our country, which is developing day by day, is facing the world.

Student 4: - Yes, you are right, peace is a great blessing. Where there is peace, children's laughter resounds. Life flourishes. Today we salute our military soldiers who protect our peace. Thanks to them, the mornings are peaceful in our country.

Leader 1:- Each country forms its own army in order to ensure its security and maintain the country's peace. The Armed Forces of the Republic of Uzbekistan were established on January 14, 1992.

Reading 1:- Article 125 of the Constitution of the Republic of Uzbekistan states that "The Armed Forces of the Republic of Uzbekistan are established to protect the state sovereignty and territorial integrity of the Republic of Uzbekistan, peaceful life and security of the population." The structure of the Armed Forces and their organization are determined by law.

Student 2: - Article 126 of the Constitution of the Republic of Uzbekistan states that "the Republic of Uzbekistan has enough armed forces to ensure its security."

A student in a soldier's uniform:
I am the happiest in the world-
I have Uzbekistan.
The gardens of Eram, for example,
I have my paradise.
Won by love of country,
Mad Doro army
Shepherd boy - Shirogdain,
I have a great wrestler.
My motherland saved,
Genghis, from the Mongol tyranny.
His song shook the sky,
I have a host.

3rd student: - "Whoever wants to understand the Uzbek name, the power of the Uzbek nation, its unlimited potential, its contribution to the development of mankind, should remember the figure of Amir Temur...", he said. IAKarimov, the First President of the Republic of Uzbekistan.

4th student: - Boys have been defenders of the Motherland, a mountain on which the country rests since time immemorial. They learned the secrets of archery, javelin, and shooting since childhood.

(The students recite Miraziz Azam's poem "Pospons of Uzbekistan")

1- presenter: - Today, our brave, brave brothers are serving their duty as young men in the ranks of the Armed Forces. Thanks to them, peace prevails in our country.

Leader 2: - During the years of independence, our army was improved in all aspects. The most modern military equipment and equipment were provided, all conditions were created for the soldiers.

1 - starter: - The Armed Forces of the Republic of Uzbekistan consist of Ground Forces, Air Defense Forces, Air Force, Special Forces and other military forces.

2 - presenter: - It is clear from this that our powerful army can reliably protect the borders of our country, our country in every way.

Reader: Holy duty - Motherland,
To protect with strength.
An independent country - body and soul,
Mehr-u ont-la to protect.

Student: Motherland day and night,
It's not easy to stand in line.
In a free, prosperous country
Ride carefully.

Reader: - Even in the hadiths, it is mentioned that one cannot protect the country without loving it, it is necessary to love it from the heart, and this is one of the main foundations of

peace. After all, loving the country is a matter of faith.
(Proverbs are said by students)

1st student: Motherland is sacred, its every elder is dear.
Student 2: Your country is peaceful - you are peaceful.
3rd student: Peacefully, the hand is blue.
The earth turns green with rain.
Student 4: You will change when you build a country.
If you don't, you will be fine.
Student 5: The power of El is real power,
Homeland is expensive.

1 - presenter: - Unfortunately, there are evil people who do not see the development, freedom, prosperity of our country. Our compatriots and the guardians of our country died bravely in several terrorist acts they carried out in order to destroy our peaceful life. These people were literally defenders of the Motherland. Their bright memory will live forever in our hearts. We are proud of them.

Reader: Our border passes through rocks and fields,
Maybe an enemy is lurking somewhere below.
Those who betray the country do not achieve their intentions,
Boundaries are strong, nothing can pass.
Reader: Border guards are the bravest guys,
His heart is fire, he is an eagle.
Sensitivity, dexterity is the most necessary quality,
Those who love their country are happy.

1 - presenter: - Our independent Uzbekistan is armed It is an honor and a sacred duty for every child to serve in the ranks of their forces. In order to become a brave soldier, we need to get deep knowledge, do sports and train. That's the only way we will become real guardians of the country.

Everyone: Today we are a perfect generation,
He is the support of this country.
If Azim is a maple, the Motherland,
We are his eyes and leaves.

2 - presenter: - May you have a blessed holiday, ever-vigilant guardians of Uzbekistan on the way to the peace of the country.

(Everyone together sings the song: "I will definitely become a sergeant").

1 - presenter: - Dear guests, dear teachers. Wishing you all health and happiness, we will end our festive evening on the occasion of the Day of the Defenders of the Fatherland.

2 - presenter: - May our homeland be peaceful and our sky be clear. May our brave boys who protect the peace of our motherland always be safe!

MARCH 8 - INTERNATIONAL WOMEN'S DAY

"BOW TO MY MOTHER"

Leader 1: Hello, old and young of the circle,
Guest and companion of the circle.
Obeisance and words to dear teachers,
Greetings to you, my peers.

Leader 2: Hello teachers! Loving thoughts,
His heart is the sun, his heart is rivers.
Dear guests,
We say hello with our hands on our chests.

1st presenter: - Hello, respected teachers, distinguished guests, loving parents, sisters and brothers and dear students of our school.

2nd host: - Welcome to today's artistic musical event called "Obeisance to my mother"!

Host 1: Today is a special world,
Today is a special day.
Today is like the sun in your eyes,
A taut knot in the morning glory.

Host 2: This morning she is wearing a satin dress,
As pink as the girls wrapped in the dawn.
The little boy who opened his eyes for the first time,
Dates are waiting for this day.

Leader 1: - "The attitude towards women should serve as a measure of the moral maturity of our society. Taking care of the mother and her child is the sacred duty of our state," said the President of the Republic of Uzbekistan.

2nd presenter: - After Uzbekistan gained independence, attention and care for women in our society is increasing year by year. Protection of their interests has risen to the level of state policy.

Leader 1: - **After all,** how much we glorify mothers who bring us all into this bright world, raise them to adulthood, and give their lives to their children.

Host 2: Greetings to you, bow to you,

Greetings to you.
We say to you from the bottom of our hearts,
Respect is a poetic word.
Leader 1: Dear mothers, lovely sisters,
May the dream come true on Independence Day.
If you walk on the stones, let the flowers spread,
May you be blessed with happiness.
(Dance will be performed by students)

Leader 1: - Well, what do you say about our mothers who rock the world with one hand and the cradle with one hand?

1- reader: How great, how dignified the mother is!

2- student: Woman! First of all, he is as great as his motherland!

3- reader: From mothers, the mountains got their dignity, the sun absorbed the temperature, and the flowers learned to smile.

4- reader: His soulful sentence is able to warm the world.

5- student: Mothers! You are the river of love, the rock of our hearts, the joy of our hearts, the light of our eyes.

6- reader: Mothers. The more we talk about you, the less it seems.

7- Reader: Language fails to describe you.

8- reader: Mother is in the sky of life
Shine like a bright sun,
 If necessary for the child,
You can even keep coal in the palm of your hand
Is there anything dearer than a mother in this world.
Every home with a mother is dear.

9- Reader: The building is filled with blood,
Propeller over the head.
For the peace of his child,
 A restless mother.
Is there anything dearer than a mother in this world?

Every home with a mother is dear.
10- reader: At the feet of his child,
A thorn if accidentally entered.
First of all, it's a good mother,
They are stabbing in the heart.
Is there anything dearer than a mother in this world?
Every home with a mother is dear.
11- reader: There is no sun in this world,
Glory is evident in your name.
Take a thousand worries,
You have shown encouragement.
12- Reader: Human life is a different tone
It sounds sometimes sad, sometimes happy
Be strong in fights
A breed that comes before the eyes.
13- Reader: Be happy in pain or sorrow,
A soul that is struggling.
It pours from the lips only,
Your dear name is mother.
14- student: Looking at mother from infancy
Looking at your tireless hardworking father
If your parents tell you to do it
It is necessary for a child to be polite.
Leader 1: Honor the woman, rub it in your eyes,
His very clean fingers.
Honor the woman, wipe the tears,
The cheeks of God.
Leader 2: Treat the woman with respect,
Ayama is the jewel of the earth.
Be brave like Shirozi, give her peace,
The most beautiful cities in the world.
1st presenter: - Woman - mother, Woman educator, Woman coach. It is because of these virtues that a woman brings up a complete and perfect person. In his wisdom, teachings, and advices, the truth of the world shines.

2nd presenter: - Humanity will not be deprived of spirituality and enlightenment even because there are intelligent women of every era.

1st presenter: Ancestor from the bosom of the grass,
Loved ones who like what I say.
Great ones like Bor, Tomaris, Uvaisi,
The women of one Parivash Uzbeg.
(Students recite poems about mothers)

2nd host: - All the beauty in life belongs to women, mothers. Because Allah made it beautiful. He took love from the sun, light from the moon, loyalty from the earth, beauty from the stars and gave it to him.

Leader 1: Always be happy for us, you are the reason why there is life, there is happiness and joy. May all of us be blessed with joy, feminine happiness, the throne of a mistress, and the kingdom of motherhood!

Leader 2: If it's good, it's worthless
A word is colorless when repeated
In this bright world, the Motherland is one,
The name mother in one world.

(Songs are performed by students, dance is performed)

1st presenter : -Dear mothers, participants of our evening! Today, as we conclude our artistic evening called "Obeisance to Mother", we wish to the Creator that you will be blessed with the sweet happiness of seeing your children grow up.

Leader 2: - May your good intentions be answered. Laugh from your lips, smile from your face!

MARCH 21 - NAVROZ HOLIDAY

"HELLO, NOWROZ"

The place of the event is very beautiful, festively decorated. In a word - the breath of spring has become a dargah reflecting the Navruz song. Singing of singers, chirping of birds, smiles on the faces of the participants of the event, good mood invite everyone to a joyful day. The song slowly fades and the announcers appear on stage. They are accompanied by a leader in two directions:

go ho come ho
I'm sorry, yes
Road rule?
come quickly
Find the way.
come play

Come to be happy, they say as if they are cheering Navroz:

Heralds: - People are people,
Almonds grown in the garden.
Don't say I didn't hear
Those who hear, do not smile,
All good people,
Come quickly to the feast.
He-he-he-hey-y!
(Enter two ushers.)
Host 1: Grassy awakening in nature today,
Dreams enter the heart with light.
Hearts are full of joy, queen,
Soft laughs moving from lips to lips.
Leader 2 : The sun enters every house,
Let it rain today.
The smile of the sun is enough for the world,
Those are the dreams in the heart today.
1st presenter : - Hello, dear teachers, distinguished guests, dear students! Navroz, the bride of the seasons, the

spring holiday has arrived in our country. Spring water freezes in streams. Budding birds, wandering in the branches of trees, nest without taking turns. The foothills, the shepherd's pastures, the gardener's garden are clothed with green grass

Leader 2 : - Yes, brides are looking for a band from chuchmoma for their hyacinth hair. Pots are hung, people are bustling. Soft sounds like a mother's voice are heard. In short, everything is refreshing. Because it is traveling along our Navruzolka. Happy Navruz!

1 - **presenter:** Indeed, Navruz is a holiday of rejuvenating and rejuvenating. Witnessing the awakening of nature is the beginning of a new day. To start our celebration today, a word to the principal of our school.

Speaker 2: " Nawroz" is a Persian word meaning "new day". March 21, the equinox of day and night, is widely celebrated by Eastern peoples as a new day, the beginning of a new year - Navruz holiday. It coincides with the beginning of planting work for farmers. This is how our great thinker grandfather A. Navoi describes this day.

I saw Vasli aro, he has the same height and hair
Navroz is now dead as night is day.

Speaker 1: Spring and woman are called twins. Therefore, our performances about mothers and women are included in our program.

Dear mothers, welcome to our breath-taking circle.

Leader 2: Dimok breathed mints,
Smallpox laughs in the heart,
A leech bride comes to say hello,
Head to the threshold, my dear guest,
Merry Christmas, my Uzbekistan

Student 1: On the moon in the sky,
Spreading like a stream,
He gave grace to our age
 Greetings to mothers.

Student 2: Our faces are blooming,
Our knowledge is abundant,

Educated,
A thousand greetings to the teachers.
Student 3: Those who wear satin dresses,
Those who served on the run,
He taught agility
Greetings to the cheerful girls.
Student 4: Those who gathered for the holiday,
Poem-song lovers,
He led the event
Greetings to the artists.
5th student: His black eye is like a bead,
Mindful of the lesson - like a hug.
Nowruz has come to school!
Greetings to all of you!

Leader 1: Let's invite Baharoi to our circle. Thank you, spring. (Spring is coming, "Spring Waltz" is playing in a low voice. Spring is coming with colorful flowers from the basket)

Spring: The season of beauty begins with spring,
It is the first morning of the year in the world.
Nowruz is happy and prosperous
The human race deserves happiness

- Hello, dear guests. I sincerely congratulate you on Navruz holiday. May the great ayam bring blessings to our country. I wish you a long, happy life and always good health.

- Girls weave flower scarves,
Do it yourself
Zamin wears a new dress
Nowruz is coming, nowruz is coming.
Lovely girls, girls,
Please feel free to write.
Happy birthday to all my people,
Nowruz is coming, nowruz is coming.

1- **host:** Let's watch the dance of our girls, dear friends. (Dances to the spring waltz.)

Leader 2: Now we invite our dearest guest Navruzjan to our circle. We all say "Hello, Navruz, welcome to our circle".

Where did we start? One, two, three...

All together: Assalam, Navroz. Welcome to our circle!

(A schoolboy in the form of Navruz, wearing a turban and a cap, enters the stage with his hand on his chest.)

Nowruz: People are people,
Almonds grown in the garden.
The winter sadness is gone from the heart,
Everyone has reached Nowruz.

ring the bell
Dancer, ayla khirom.
During this holiday season,
Rest in peace everyone.

May the spring day, which has covered the world with flowers, be blessed, dear ones. This spring is not just a season, it is the spring of everyone's life. I see the freshness of spring in all faces.

Student 1: (*Poem: " Happy Navrozim from your letter"*)
The snow is melting on the ground,
There is no limit to my joy, I observed myself.
Have you come to the way we have been waiting for, spring?
Happy New Year!

We've been waiting for you, we've been waiting for you,
You are happy for the holidays - this is my sincere word,
The epic that sings you - many songs,
Happy New Year.

Leader 2: Dear friends, let's listen to Navroz song now. *(The song plays.)*

1 - starter. Navruzjan, do you know wonderful people who celebrate this day as a labor holiday, when you roll up your sleeves and go to work?

Nowruz: The first one is Dehkan Baba. Here they are

visiting.

Spring and Navruz accompanied: - Hello, my grandfather farmer,
My light boston, whose generosity is unlimited.
Don't you think it's Labor Day?
My whole world bows to you.

(A young man in peasant clothes enters the circle. He greets the guests with his hand on his chest.)

Grandfather Farmer: Plowing without stopping,
A double ox with a farmer.
Our destiny will be complete
Nowruz is coming, nowruz is coming.
Oh God, take care of yourself
Do not let the evil eye touch you.
May the souls of my aunts be happy,
Nowruz is coming, nowruz is coming.

- Yes, dear ones, Navruz is a holiday of goodness. On this day, whoever sets his mind will definitely achieve it. If you listen to the prayers of young and old, they ask the Creator to bless agriculture. After all, our sustenance and destiny is behind this farming.

Leader 2: Navrozi world has arrived,
The pen is weak for drawing.
If I weave a thousand and one songs,
All in all, there is little.
A carpet spread out
You are so beautiful

1st presenter : On the occasion of Nowruz, special dishes and sweets are prepared and the festive table is decorated. That is, sumalak, halim, blue somsa, blue dumplings, dolma, gursok for the Nowruz table. are the main dishes. The idea of putting "Navroz Goja" on the spring holiday table in Khorezm there is The parable of Navruz Goja consists of 7 different grains. Oats, wheat , agra , millet, rice , beans and mush .

Speaker 2: Sumac is one of the best spring foods. In the early morning, sumac put in pots is boiled and cooked for a day and a night.

Student: You are screaming and boiling,
We will die if we stir it up.
You won't let us stir,
Sumalakjon, sumalak.
One night and one day,
We do not smile around you.
A star sleeps in the sky,
We don't know how to sleep.
Let the fairy tales be gone,
Squealing stones.
Leads to fortitude,
Endure the fire.
Incite intention
A custom from my ancestors.
Be with my people, comrade,
Always happy.
(Students perform the song "Sumalak".)

Leader 1: Traditions, customs, and customs play an important role in human development. They appeared due to vital necessity and greatly influenced the spiritual and moral development of the society by expressing the wishes of the people's lifestyle, psyche, and spiritual world. Now it's time for Nowruz udums.

Student 1: They clean the house on Navroz.

2nd student: Until Nowruz, the trees whiten their trunks.

Student 3: In Nowruz, they collect wheat and cook sumak.

4th student: They make good intentions in Navroz.
5th student: They wear new clothes on Navroz.
6th student: They cook Navruz dishes on Navruz.

Leader 1: Nowruz is a spiritual mirror that clearly

shows to the world whose descendants we are, and what kind of great heritage we are inheritors.

As the cranes return to their land,
Your money is returning to your bosom.
It gives a dreamy look from Moziy
Thank you, congratulations, your greatness!
My boston that gave great geniuses,
Happy New Year, my Uzbekistan!

Starter 2: I am blessed in my land,
Navrozi world is visiting.
special right reigns in the hearts,
Across the country the festive spirit is on the move.

1st **speaker** : May Nowruz bring peace, safety,
A rich table h a m prosperity.
congratulations to all of us Happy birthday, friends! Happy Nowruz holiday!

MAY 9 - DAY OF MEMORY AND APPRECIATION

"THE MOST HOLY DAY"

The place of the event should be decorated in accordance with the day of remembrance, full of impressions. The room is hung with pictures of those who died in the Second World War, the memory of the victims of repression, and the elderly fathers and mothers who are living their old age. Among them, a large photo of the First President with the youth stands out.

Teacher: - Hello, dear students who have gathered for our evening, teachers who have added grace to our class! Welcome! May 9th - We announce the opening of our "Holiest Day" holiday party dedicated to the Day of Remembrance and Appreciation.

1- presenter: - Memory is a sacred feeling that calls to self-awareness, to always remember the past. A person understands his identity more deeply through this memory and sense of value.

2nd presenter: - We respectfully mention words such as nation, homeland, independence. When we talk about these concepts, our mind is involuntarily occupied by a sense of memory. Human memory is sacred. That is why we remember our ancestors and remember their good deeds.

1st presenter: - Sacred concepts are actually alive with memory. It means not only not forgetting the past, but also vividly imagining the present and the future.

Leader 2: - Memory teaches a person to look into the future with deep eyes.

1- presenter: - Appreciation is the respect of our luminaries, who are the pillars of our family, who bless our homes and wish us white blessings in our work . Besides, great wisdom is hidden in people's appreciation of each other.

Student 1: You are my grandfather, Khatira
You are my mother, Qadr.

A long ways-a ... Memory ...
A long way... Appreciation...
Student 2: The mountains of the whirling world,
Po'panak connects rakhtma - rakht.
Memory is the stain of my heart,
Qadr is a tree on which my heart rests
Student 3: I am from the same branch, Qadr
You are my grandfather, Khatira.
You are my mother, Qadr,
A long way-a Memory.
(Congratulations.)

Leader 1: - As much as our forefathers took care of their families and women, they also took care of the Motherland.

2nd presenter: - "There is no future without historical memory," said the First President. We also use the word value next to the word memory. What for? Because Memory and Qadr cannot live without each other. We want these two noble feelings not to be far away from any of us. May it always echo in our hearts.

VIEW OF THE STAGE

A sad tune is playing. The music goes down, and a student in the person of our favorite poet, the late Muhammad Yusuf, appears on the stage

- Hello, dear guests, respected teachers, smart students! You are a child of an independent country, a bright future of a free Motherland. You also have a huge contribution in making our dreams come true. Never forget us.

Tickling my sad memory today,
You caused a bright feeling.
Your soul flies over your head day and night,
You help me in every good work.
Memory is sacred, Memory is eternal!

Puchmok has gone to the depths of history,

Neither scholars nor heroes.
Each of them is sealed,
Indelible memories in the hearts of the people.
Memory is sacred, Memory is eternal!

(The song "Qadiry Babam" by the poet Muhammad Yusuf will be performed)

1st leader: - Every day hundreds of pilgrims visit the memorial square in our capital.

2nd presenter: - There is a person who has stepped into the field of memory and will not leave without impressions and surprises. Some people get tears in their eyes when they see the name of their loved one in the book of memory, while others are thankful that they have reached these days. Motamsaro calling for peace Wreaths at the base of the mother statue filled with All this is an expression of respect for the souls of the departed.

(A small scene will be shown during the visit of the students to the memory area)

Leader 1: - The students of our school came to visit this auspicious place under the leadership of their teachers.

Student 1: - Our teacher took us to the Memorial Square. During the visit, we talked with a father.

Nurani Atakhan: - Our youth was spent in battles, in the depths of the fire of war. Here we are over ninety. Thankfully, we live in drug-free times. We gained value thanks to independence. This shrine was built in honor of you, our dear children, our countrymen who fought for a happy, peaceful life and the freedom of the Motherland. Peace is a great blessing, we should appreciate it. We, the elderly, pray for you. Because you are happy children of an independent country enjoying the care of our President.

2nd student: - After the father's words, we understood that we need to reach the value of peace and tranquility even more.

1st leader: - The names of nearly a thousand of our compatriots who sacrificed their lives in the battlefields are written in the Book of Remembrance. At the initiative of the

First President, the names of 3,725 more compatriots were identified and recorded in this book.

Leader 2: - The purpose of holding the Day of Remembrance and Appreciation is to perpetuate the memory of our nation's children who sacrificed their lives for the freedom and independence of the Motherland, to honor the veterans who contribute to the development of our country today.

Leader 1:- It should be said that this is not only a commemoration of those who died on the battlefield, but also a commemoration of people who selflessly worked behind the front, in the years after the war, and contributed to our medical days.

2- presenter: - Distinguished guests, dear teachers, dear students! With this, we will conclude our event dedicated to the Day of Remembrance and Appreciation, and we wish that the concepts of Remembrance and Appreciation will not leave any of you.

Host 1: Mint, looking for traces of basil,
I want the stars like the fourteen-day moon.
To awake generations, like an awake soul,
I am talking about their lives.
To the martyrs of the great freedom,
I restored the marble slabs from my heart.
Today to the martyrs of independence,
Let them talk about the love of the country.
Starter 2: Again in the lists of compatriots,
They live as living people.
In the boundaries of honesty and justice,
They start the year with a bright day.
They are the stainless gold of value,
Unfading stars in the constellation of memory.
Every spring blooms before the gardens,
 They are evergreen roots.
(The night ends with soft music.)

II. SCENARIOS OF THE EVENTS DEDICATED TO THE BIRTH DATES OF THE GREAT SOLUTIONS OF THE HISTORY AND LITERATURE OF THE UZBEK PEOPLE

FEBRUARY 9 - THE BIRTHDAY OF THE GREAT THINKER ALLAMA ALISHER NAVOY

"A CONTEMPORARY IMAGE FOR THE TIMES"

The classroom or school hall will be beautifully decorated. A picture of Alisher Navoi is hung on the wall, and information about the poet's works is placed around it. Pictures drawn by students dedicated to Navoi's work will also be hung. Under the sound of music, presenters and participants of the event will appear on the stage.

Teacher: - Hello, dear teachers, respected parents, dear guests who visited our event! Today is the 582nd anniversary of the birth of Alisher Navoi, a great scholar and poet. Welcome to our event called "A contemporary figure for the times" organized to celebrate this date!

("Aziz boston-Uzbekistan" composed to the poetry of Minhojeddin Mirzo and the music of Dilorom Omonullayeva will be performed with the accompaniment of singers and the event will begin).

1st presenter: We are Uzbek youth, wordsmiths,
This is the dream of Turonn of old,
Sometimes it's a calm river, sometimes it's raging
We tremble even on the lawn,
Homeland, we will be Tomaris, Shirak.

2nd presenter: All four seasons are flower garden, flower garden season,
All four seasons are the Motherland, ours is the original,
A perfect offspring of a perfect generation,
The mountains will be the hands of the boys!
Motherland, we will be the heart that beats for you!
(A photo of Alisher Navoi is shown through a slide

under the sound of music.)

Leader 1: Years pass, centuries pass
New generations are coming to the world
But history does not forget,
Great ancestors who lived as Elim.
Starter 2: A boston full of navo and magic
Boston is always beautiful, summer and winter
Gardener Hazrat Navoi Erur
Each time there will be one new word.
Today, another young man named Navoi
Navoi lives in the hearts of generations.
Leader 1: Besh asrkim, nazmi saroyni
A lion in chains trembles.
Where Temur's blade did not reach
Alisher took it with a pen.

- Our great-grandfather Alisher Navoi is truly inscribed in the history of mankind with the name of the Sultan of speech. He was born on February 9, 1441 in the city of Herat. From a young age, he loved books and grew up to be polite and intelligent. He wrote many ghazals, epics and rubai. Ever since he was a child, he memorized the entire work of Fariduddin Attar and surprised many with his talent.

Leader 2: Loud - I speak loudly,
Vazmin, I will think carefully.
I will paint the skies
When I read Navoi.

- Now let's give the turn to the students, they will tell the ghazals and rubai they learned from the works of the great poet.

(Several students go on the stage and sing verses and ghazals, wise words from the works of Alisher Navoi).

Student 1: Body is a common word
The word is effective for the soul.
Student 2: A stranger in a foreign land cannot be happy,
El anga shafiq-u is not kind.
The golden cage is filled with red flower shoes,

Bulbulga is a sucker like a thorn.

Student 3: You don't care about the language - you don't care about it.

Student 4: Put your head on the spoon,
Make your body almsgiving.
The light that turns into your night and day,
One is the moon, the other is the sun.
Except for the pen that does not smoke from the words,
Do not step outside of the letters.

Student 5: A scientist who learns what he does not know by asking, a tyrant who does not ask.

Student 6: Little by little, one becomes wise, and one by one, one becomes a river.

Lesson 7: Don't waste your life, work hard, Know that work is the key to your happiness.

8th student: Know the word Donau dur as a legend, Know the word as a masterpiece in the world.

1st host: - Our grandfather Alisher Navoi is the founder of the Uzbek language, isn't that right, comrade?

Leader 2: - Yes, of course. Like our grandfather, we must preserve our language. The fact that the Uzbek language is the state language is also established in our Constitution. Please read this article.

(Student 1 comes out and introduces Article 4 of the Constitution of the Republic of Uzbekistan. The Constitution of the Republic of Uzbekistan is shown on the slide.)

(3 students and the image of Navoi (a student in the form of Navoi) appear on the stage)

1st student:- Dear grandfather! You are unique and eternal. The works you created are clear as the sky, clear as the dawn, and mixed with musical tones.

While reading your works, it is not difficult to realize that you are one soul, one body with your people, humanity, from every line of yours.

Don't leave your country for a breath,

Don't be angry and jealous again.

2nd student: - Dear grandfather! You seem to be revealing the magic of words, the meaning of life, and the door of happiness to humanity with your attractive verses. In this Gulshan, you have shown that the key to happiness is doing good to people.

This flower is full of frogs.

Ajab saad erur good if it comes out.

3rd student: - Great teacher! You are the sultan of the ghazal estate. You for life:

If you are a human, you are not a human.

The grief of a people without mine, -

You stayed true to your motto.

(students leave)

Voice:

The world has seen what is holy,

You are the mother of all, O powerful life.

Looking down from the depths of the ages,

A bright breed for these bright faces.

Honor this great son of yours from the heart,

My people, it's enough to bow down.

Signed with his name

Uzbek name in the world register.

(A classic tune is played. Navoi is in his studio.....)

The cypress flower didn't come yesterday.

My eyes did not sleep until dawn yesterday.

I'm waiting on the way to the end of the moment,

He did not come to my mouth.

(gradually the figure of Navoi withdraws from the stage and joins the song and dance. Munojot.)

1st presenter : - Now it's the turn of the students to present a scene called "Mir Alisher and the Sick Man". Thank you.

(From the book "El desa Navoiyni". Compiler: M. Jorayev).

While Mir Alisher Navoi was reading a book on stage, a man came to him and complained about his poor health:

- Mawlana Mir Alisher, you are a wise man, a poet, a just emir, but it's too bad that you don't know about medicine.

Mir Alisher Navoi: - Where does it hurt?

Sick man: - I don't even know, I have pain everywhere, but I have no heat in my body.

Mir Alisher Navoi: - In that case, there is a cure. One prayer time in the morning, one more prayer time in the evening, and the rest of the time, do your work, insha'Allah, you will recover quickly...

1st presenter: - After a few days, a man again came to Mir Alisher.

- Do you recognize me, sin?

Mir Alisher Navoi: I met you, but how is your health?

Sick man: - I am a horse. Even though a poet is a healer, I did what you said and got rid of the pain completely. (Satisfied look).

1st presenter: - Dear readers, our grandfather Mir Alisher Navoi was a very intelligent person, besides being educated. Don't be like the sick person in our scene. Don't get tired of working and learning.

2nd leader : - It is the turn of our students, they will read samples of poems written by Tursunboy Adashboyev, Khurshid Davron and Abdulla Oripov dedicated to Alisher Navoi.

(Students read the poems expressively)

Speaker 1: We rightly call the thinker Allama A. Navoi "a contemporary figure of the times". Because his life, all his work and creativity are relevant at all times. At this point, let us quote the definitions given to this great breed by the honorable First President of the Republic of Uzbekistan, IAKarimov.

(The monitor shows: "If we call him a saint, he is the saint of saints, if we say a thinker, he is a thinker of thinkers, if we say a poet, he is a sultan of poets."

2nd leader: - Here are students, dear guests and parents. Today's event has come to an end. We are descendants of world-famous ancestors! Remembering their memory, we should grow up to be worthy of them and contribute to the development of the Motherland. For this, we need to grow up, learn the way of life of our great-grandfathers and follow their example. Let's draw a conclusion from the event (slide): knowing Navoi means knowing oneself, loving Navoi means loving the nation, loyalty to Navoi means loyalty to the most noble human values.

The caravans of the ages passing one after the other,
Oh, how dangerous are its great passes,
It was enough for the human race for ages.
At least the dreams of the hopeful Navoi come true.
The opportunity has come, this is the day to know who my friend is.
This is the day that I wish blessings to all the children of mankind,
this is the day when I look at the sky and make supplications at dawn,
my dear grandfather, may the spaces of Navoi be filled with light.

FEBRUARY 14 - ZAHRIDDIN MUHAMMAD BABUR'S BIRTHDAY

"THEN MY LIFE REMAINS MINE"

The stage is decorated in a festive spirit. The portrait of Zahriddin Muhammad Babur, as well as works of the poet, booklets are on the grid. There are posters with excerpts from his poems and rubai. (A song based on the poet's ghazal "Yakhshiliq" will be played. Two presenters will appear on the stage).

Leader 1: Ancient - my endless epic from ancient times,
My beautiful boston, looking down on the truth,
The land of the Alpomish is my bright place,
Hello, my motherland, Uzbekistan!
Leader 2: I have not seen Tanti el, my people like you,
I did not see sweet words, my people like you,
I have not seen a pure heart, my people like you,
Hello, my motherland, Uzbekistan!
1- **presenter:** - A star flying from Andijan's bosom,
A beaver is like a jewel in India's crown.
A word swirls in the heart of fire,
Anda there is a soul left, there is a soul left.
Leader 2: The world spins endlessly,
Troubled times will pass.
A word groans from the depths of the ages,
There is a soul left, there is a soul left.

Leader 1: - Hello Hello, dear teachers, dear parents and dear students! Today, we intend to bring to your attention our spiritual-educational event called "Anda jonim zhali mening", prepared on the occasion of the 540th anniversary of the birth of the king and poet, statesman and great general Zahriddin Muhammad Babur.

2nd leader: - Zahriddin Muhammad Babur was born on February 14, 1483 in Andijan in the house of Umarshaikh

Mirza. After the death of his father, Babur, who received a proper education typical of princes in the palace, ascended the throne at the age of 12.

Leader 1: -Babur left Andijan due to the wars for the throne and founded the great Babur dynasty in India. Our beloved poet, who established a powerful kingdom in India and contributed greatly to the country's prosperity, died in Agra in 1530.

2nd presenter: - During his lifetime, he created many prose and poetic works such as "Baburnoma", "Mubbayin al-zakot" ("Description of Zakat"), "Hatti Baburiy", "Harb ishi".

(Students go on the stage and one by one they say from Babur's Rubaiyat).

1st presenter: - The era passed me by saru samondin,
He took me away from me.
Sometimes it's a stone on my head, sometimes it's a curse.
It didn't occur to me for a while.

Leader 2: - You don't get involved in everything,
This means that you will not reach your goal.

1st presenter: - Someone is disappointed with someone,
One hundred words make a person happy.

2 - host: - You don't remember the person who sucks
A person who sucks the heart out of work is not happy
My heart did not die happily in this strangeness
There is certainly a person who does not rejoice in a foreign country.

1 - the leader: - How much do you obey your ego,
What a waste of your life.

1st student: - Even though Babur was a king in India, he missed his country, its land, and its people all his life.

2nd student: - He is different He thought that a piece of land of his homeland was better than the throne of the country and he lived with this dream. We feel the longing for the Homeland, which has become a dream in the poet's ghazals and rubai.

VIEW OF THE STAGE

(Soft music is playing. Babur is sitting on the throne. He is talking with three or four of his attendants about the political situation in the country and taxes. Then a special guard comes and says that a man is asking permission to enter Babur's presence.)

Babur: - Please bring it to me!

(A stranger enters with a melon in his hand and bows)

Person: - Hello, my lord. *(Obeisance is performed)*. I am a merchant. The purpose of my coming to you is that I brought you a melon brought from Andijan. Taste this bounty from your homeland, my lord. If Zora is a balm for your longing. *(Babur slowly descends from the throne and takes the melon with trembling hands. He sniffs it for a long time and rubs it on his face and eyes and speaks very sadly.)*

Babur: - Thank you. In this melon, which brought the beauty of my country, I felt the wind and clean air of Andijan, the warmth of the fertile soil, the beauty of the incomparable fields, the scenery of the beautiful valleys where I spent my childhood, the breath of my kind people, the love of my parents. The Motherland, where my navel blood was spilled, is my cradle, longing, and endless dream. *(Hazin recites rubai in a melodious tone)*.

There is no tole, my soul has become a child,
I did everything - there was a mistake.
I left my country and turned to India,
Yarab, netayin, ne face blackness.

(After that, S. Nazarkhan's song "Ulugimsan, Watanim" will be played. Babur, who was overwhelmed by the song, his servants, and then the merchant, will slowly leave the stage).

Leader 1: My people, your great son, your great royal son,

A dream remained in Babur's heart.
Be patient with the burning lamentation,
Is there a soul left?

Leader 2: Let everyone have their own shelter
Let everyone spend their time in their huts.
I'm not talking about people in this world
Even a bird's nest in a foreign branch.

1st presenter: -Zahriddin Muhammad Babur was a great talent who produced works in Turkish and Persian languages. He created beautiful works in such genres as rubai, tuyuq, qita, masnavi, fard. He collected them and formed two - "Indian Cabinet" and "Kabul Cabinet". But "Kabul Divan" has not been found yet.

2nd presenter: - Babur occupies a special place in our literature with his rubai with deep philosophical meaning. The perfect expression of inner experiences, sometimes happy, sometimes sad moods in four lines shows that he is a sharp rubeologist poet.

Student 1: Whoever is faithful is faithful,
Anyone who punishes will be punished.
It's bad if a good person doesn't see it,
Anyone who is bad is punished.

Student 2: Please give me more, I have nowhere to go.
I don't have a decision for a moment or a breath.
I came here of my own free will,
But I have no choice.

1st presenter: - The poetry of the great poet Zahriddin Muhammad Babur has a great place in our literature due to its rare and artistic value. His work "Boburnoma" is recognized worldwide as an invaluable historical work of art.

1st presenter: - Our beloved writer Pirimkul Kadirov's historical novels such as "Starry Nights" or "Babur", "Avlodlar Dovani", "Humayun and Akbar" are about the life and work of our beloved poet Babur, representatives of the powerful kingdom he founded in India - the Babur dynasty. can provide a wide range of historical information. As we read these works, our love for our great poet grows even more.

2nd host: Andijan is a world that is bruised in my heart
The puddles on my way
misses me even if i don't
Dandelions in Bogi Babur.

Leader 1: Take care of your own seedlings
You are not tall enough, nor are you tall enough
If a king comes out of your child - a king in another country
If the poet comes out, he will leave.

Leader 2: If you see the deeds of the unfaithful world,
An Indian guest chooses the palace you have built
Maybe if you're fit, if you're a little wider
Tajimahals would be in your lap.

-Dear guests and readers, today's event dedicated to the birthday of king and poet Babur has come to an end.

(The evening will end with the continuation of Babur's song "Yakhshiliq").

FEBRUARY 9- BIRTHDAY OF SAHIBQIRAN AMIR TEMUR

"OUR OWNER'S GRANDPA"

The stage will be decorated in the national spirit. A portrait of our grandfather is placed in the middle. The following comments about Amir Temur are displayed on the monitor:

"This classic figure, a symbol of unparalleled determination, bravery and wisdom, built a great kingdom and left a practical and theoretical legacy in terms of statecraft. It opened a wide path for the development of science, culture, creativity, religion and spirituality."

(IA Karimov.)

Host 1: O land that told me tales,
I will follow your footsteps.
The garden of Eram in the eyes of others,
I can't take you to the leaf of Jiydang.
Homeland, you are always my companion.
You are my place of worship where my ancestors lie.
Leader 2: Singing over the golden cradle,
I am always awake.
Jilgasi slang wakes up in the morning.
The spring that came to my heart,
Homeland, you are always my companion.
You are my place of worship where my ancestors lie.
1st presenter: - Hello, dear and kind teachers! Dear parents and guests of our circle! Welcome to our spiritual and educational evening dedicated to the 687th anniversary of the birth of our grandfather Amir Temur!
2nd host: Uzbek is worth being proud of,
Perhaps in the high glory of a breed.
Temurbek's star is like a golden pile,
The lights are in the sky of the great ones.
Leader 1: Wow, a chain palace alone
The one who was able to take revenge from the Horde.

A large place called Turon,
He couldn't hold it for so many years.

1st student: - Amir Temur is a great person, a great leader, a great statesman, a jurist, a skilled architect, an orator, a spiritualist, at the same time, a person who loved his country and made him famous around the world.

2nd student: - Our grandfather, Amir Temur, was born on April 9, 1336, in the Khoja Ilgor village of the ancient city of Kesh, in the family of Taragay Bahadir and Tagina. His full name is Amir Temur Ibn Amir Taragai ibn Amir Barqul.

3rd student: - His father, Amir Taragai, was a wealthy man. Temur's youth and young manhood were spent in a period when the country was in a difficult situation.

3rd reader:- According to the famous historian Sharafiddin Ali Yazdi, Chistan is a powerful slave of the governor, and the governor mobilizes our brave and courageous grandfather Amir Temur to fight with him. Our grandfather leads his men and goes into battle. At that time, Amir Temur was seriously injured in the right hand and right leg. This event happened in 1364.

4th student:- Our grandfather's services to history are incomparable. He will end the growing disunity in the country and unite the country under his flag. It forms the basis of a large centralized state.

5th student:- This creates a solid foundation for the development of agriculture, crafts, trade and culture.

6th student:- Today, the words "Timur and Timurid State", "Timurian Culture", "Ulugbek and Samarkand School of Astrology", "Babur", "Babur Empire" are not only Uzbek, but also Uzbek. as we meet in the history pages of the peoples of the whole world, we should not forget that Amir Temur's great merits are at the root of them.

7th student:- Our grandfather Amir Temur helped a number of nations and countries to be freed from the oppression of colonialists. He defeated Yildirim Bayazid (1380-1402), the most powerful king of that time, and freed European nations from captivity.

8th student:- Khan of the Golden Horde defeats Tokhtamish and accelerates the liberation of Russia from Mongol rule by almost 300 years.

9th student:- Our grandfather will turn the land of Turkestan into an advanced country where agriculture, crafts, science and culture are developed.

10th student:- Won't you tell me the cities, towns, villages that were improved by the efforts of Amir Temur, the buildings that rose in the city like Samarkand, Shahrisabz, Yassi (Turkestan)? They are now adding beauty to the beauty of our country and are standing proudly as a symbol of greatness and strength.

11th student:- During the lifetime of our grandfather, his work called "Timur's rules" dedicated to the military art and state management style gained fame.

12th student:- Our grandfather attached special importance to the beautification of the capital Samarkand for the glory of his country. He had a habit of celebrating every triumphant event, joyful event by building a magnificent architectural monument.

13th student: "If you doubt our power, look at the buildings we built!" an appeal was signed.

14th student:- Our grandfather built many beautiful gardens around Samarkand. Bogi Dilkusho, Bogi Chinor, Bogi Behisht, Bogi Baland, Bogi Nav, Davlatabad, Bogi Shamal, Bogi Jahannoma, Bogi Maidan and their beautiful boxes are high examples of horticultural art of that time.

15th student:- Our grandfather Amir Temur took important measures to ensure the safety of trade caravans on the Great Silk Road, an international trade route from China and India through Central Asia to the Middle East and European countries. 'rgan. This led to the stability of foreign-economic and diplomatic relations of Amir Temur's state.

Starter 1:
From the Mongol conquest of the world,
The rescued barlosian hero.
Unable to escape from the demands of fate,
Being named Fatih is the end of itself.
Starter 2:
The greatest buildings are statues,
There is Samarkand-ku, which has no equal in the world.
Temurbek is full of battle excitement,
He has a sword in his hand and a bundle under it.

Student 1: Bibikhanim stayed in Samarkand,
Bibikhanim looked at the roads.
Until an Uzbek makes you an Uzbek
The sultan did not dismount for forty years.
Praise and blame,
The king's dream leads to the cliff,
He did not respond to flattery,
Sultan did not fall for lies.
Although beckoning or not,
Thirty countries are under control.
A sip of pride is soft,
The sultan did not taste or drink.
2nd student: We took a spill and rebuilt another figure,
We put the burden of the nation on our shoulders.
The building became a soul for free beings,
What day did the dear words fly off the tongue?
The name Uzbek conquered the world!
This country hit its head on stones,
This land has been destroyed and rebuilt.
The architect of the Tajmahal, the son of the Nile.
This is the land of Amir Temurs.
Greetings from us to those who missed us,
The name Uzbek conquered the world!
(Said by the students from the wisdom of Amir Temur)
1. Strength is in justice.

2. If you are white, do not swear.

3. Make friends with brave people, because God honors brave people.

4. Try the good on a bad day.

5. An intelligent enemy is better than an ignorant friend.

6. One laugh of justice is better than a thousand days of obedience.

Leader 1: God bless you so much,
Kamil-u is mature family breed.
One side is Bibikhanim, the other side is Shahrukh.
On the one hand, Ulugbek is an unbreakable wing.

Leader 2: How lucky I am, when my native land is free,
You have returned to the blessed homeland.
Ignorant generation.
Thank you for watching us.

1st presenter: - On the initiative of the First President of the Republic of Uzbekistan, IAKarimov, 1996 was called the year of Amir Temur and the Order of Amir Temur was established. Statues of our grandfather have been installed in the cities of Samarkand, Tashkent, and Shahrisabz, and they are now in full bloom.

Leader 2: - The inscription "Strength is in justice" written on the ring seals of Amir Temur will be forever imprinted in the hearts of our generations and will serve as a program in our life path.

1st presenter: - We are the children of the nation who have surprised the world with their knowledge and potential, enlightenment and culture, faith, love and high spirituality. We are proud of our great grandfathers and will be their worthy successors.

III. EVENT SCENARIOS ON DIFFERENT THEMES RELATED TO MOTHER NATURE, COMMUNITY LIFE

"JOURNEY TO SPACE"

Leader : Once there is, once there is no. These days, there is a boy named Nurmuhammad in our dear country of Uzbekistan. He likes to go out into the yard at night and watch the stars in the clear sky. Nurmuhammad had a younger brother named Maqsad, and he used to listen to his brother's stories about the secrets of the stars and planets with pleasure. They have close friends named Dinora and Malika. One day, four friends made a flying horse-rocket. This rocket is not an ordinary rocket. It flies faster than sound and chases light.

(Nurmuhammad, Maqsad, Dinora and Malika enter the stage)

Dinora: Guys, look how great our rocket turned out.
Objective: What will we name our rocket?
Princess: The name we put on our rocket should be very catchy.
Nurmuhammad: Let's call our ship "Istiqlal".
Dinora: I liked it.
Goal: A great name.
Dinora: It's time to test our ship "Istiqlal".
Purpose: Yes, that's right.
Nurmuhammad: I will travel to space with Malika.
Dinora: We promise to pass on the information you sent to our peers in our motherland.
Purpose: We use a smart machine computer network for communication.
Princess: Then let's go on a journey.
Purpose: Goodbye.
Dinora: Come back safely.
(A video image of a rocket flying is shown on the screen)

Host : Let's take a look at which planets the ship

"Istiqlal" traveled to.

The 1st planet they visited was the planet Bolalik, located next to the brightest star.

Malika: Nurmuhammad, look, these are the heroes of the fairy tales we read.

Nurmuhammad: Yes, let's go to them and find out what they are arguing about.

Children: Hello.
Bilmasvoy: Who are you?
Price: Where are you from?
Little Red Riding Hood: What are you here for?
Nurmuhammad: My name is Nurmuhammad.
Princess: Mine is Princess.

Nurmuhammad: We came from the planet Earth, from a country called Uzbekistan. Our goal is to travel to space on the ship "Istiqlal" that we created.

Buratino: We have heard about this country.

(Music plays)

Nurmuhammad:
Our hardworking, tolerant compatriots,
Our knowledgeable, aspiring young people...
Our prosperous cities and villages,
Uzbekistan is the country of the lucky ones.

Princess: Every day there is a celebration in the houses,
A tradition that is a national tradition.
We say happy again and again,
Uzbekistan is the country of the lucky ones.

Don't know: There are hundreds of countries in the world,
Uzbekistan is among them.

Little Red Riding Hood: The people of that country are kind, honest,
Smiles on faces, happy hearts.

Price: In some countries, what a terrible horror,
There are wars going on.

Buratino: Peace is always in Uzbekistan,
There is only goodness in the hearts of the people.

Princess: So what are you guys arguing about?
Precious: Today is the Little Prince's birthday, and we don't know what to give him.
Little Red Riding Hood: Maybe we'll bring him some of the somsa that my mother cooked.
Buratino: No, we'll take a lamb. He loves lambs.
Bilmasvoy: After all, he has a lamb.
Nurmuhammad: Let's give him a book.
Princess: Yes, we have a wonderful fairy tale book in our rocket, we can give it away if you want.
Value: We agree, what better gift than a book?
All: Happy Birthday, Little Prince.
Little Prince: Thank you, come be my dear guest.
(Murod plays a circle, Munira dances, Kimmat joins the dance in the middle of the game)
(Nurmuhammad and Malika say goodbye to the heroes of the fairy tale.)
Host : After the party, the children said goodbye to their fairy-tale heroes and continued on their journey. The second planet they visited was the Magic Numbers planet.
Malika: Nurmuhammad, why is this planet called "Magic Numbers"?
Nurmuhammad: Come, we will find out by asking.
Princess: Why is your planet called "Magic Numbers"?
Munira: Because the world cannot be imagined without numbers. Numbers are made up of numbers. Let's get to know them.

Parizoda: Enriched the knowledge of arithmetic,
Ten is a popular number
Numbers, numbers
This world is meaningful.
Numbers are the heart of the decimal system.

It is Erur's wish to serve people.

Numbers:

One: One is the only number,
 I'm easy to count.
One heart, one head,
One moon, one sun.
Mother - Motherland - the only one,
Kurramim is also one piece.
Everyone is one,
Add up - a thousand, a million.
I'm about to write:
I look like a pile.

Ikki: My name is Ikki,
 Two one - I'm ready.
Two hands, two legs,
Two eyes, two ears.
Parents are two souls,
Both are kind.
There will be even two odd,
Know me well, friend!
What do I look like, then?
Like a swan on a lake.

Three: I am three, my name is three
There is strength in unity.
Count to three
Every lion who played the bet.
Prayer if recited three times
 It's good for us.
When it comes to three baby,
How sweet, baby!
It is not difficult to write:
Two bites...

Four: I am the number four,
 I'm a total of two.
Two pairs of comrades
Four ulfat that time.

A horse has four legs
It will be close
There are four seasons in a year,
Original from each other.
Single belt ladder,
A wrestler with his hand on his waist.
Five: I have a name that says five,
 The numbers are advanced.
If they add up one by one, I am a lot,
Five panjamans in hand.
If you always get five marks,
You will study well!
If there are five continents, comrade,
It will be quiet soon.
Good effort to write:
It's like a fishing rod.
Six: It's six after five,
 If you add two ends, then
Never leave the sedan.
Parents, four children –
Six people are a family.
Happy Six Youths,
I need to count!
Must know how to write:
A seemingly simple hook...
Seven: My name is Seven,
 Don't say you're a dwarf.
I'm one more than six
I am seven stars, I am a ball.
There will be seven days in the week
Weeks to months.
At the age of seven, of course,
You go to school.
A small scythe in Chizgin,
Belt around the waist.
Eight: Don't count and say eight,
 If you add two fours–

It will be this moment,
You know well, brother.
I am the brother of seven,
Countless numbers.
When you reach eight,
You study higher class.
Let me write
Imagine a cocoon.
Nine: I am nine, nine,
I am alone in the thighs.
One big one out of eight,
Be sure to find out.
Even if there are three in three places
This is the moment when I will be born.
Anyone who enters is nine years old
His mind is full.
Learn to write slowly:
The tail of the hook is below.
Zero: Attention, my name is Zero,
Reader, beware.
If I stand alone - I am not,
If there is a partner - I am full.
My brother is standing in front of me
I really will be great.
Ten hundred, thousand, million,
If you add, it's a big number.
Just draw a circle
It is not difficult to write me!
Afterword
Numbers conversation,
It took too long.
Each in turn
He swam proudly.
Our great grandfathers,
Scholars, sages,
Khorezmi, Al-Farghani,
Ulugbek, Koragony...

What other scientists,
Knowledge about number-
They have enriched their field.
He wrote many works.
If you are in numbers, my friend,
You will be in a good mood!
"You need to know the world,
There is a reckoning to be made!"
(Teacher and two students enter the stage)
Teacher: Hello, students.
Readers: Hello, hello.
Teacher: Today we will repeat the multiplication table with you. Come on, Nurullayeva, stand up, how much will we get if we multiply 7 by 8?
(The student thinks about the answer, asks the student next to him, does not find the answer)
Teacher: Sit down!
(Students sing the song "Don't give up, teacher" in unison.)
Teacher: Okay, I'll wait until now. Memorize it until the next lesson.
Host : Two friends Nurmuhammad and Malika invited their friends from the planet "Magic numbers" to their planet and said goodbye to them. The next planet they visited was the Rare Wealth planet. We will watch.
Nurmuhammad: Which planet is this?
Princess: Planet of "Rare Wealth".
Nurmuhammad: Why is it called that?
Princess: Come, it's better to ask and find out about it.
(The student comes out. The children greet each other.)
Princess: Is this the planet of "Rare Wealth"?
Student: Yes, it is.
Princess: Why did you name your planet like that?
Reader: Come on, think for yourself, what is this rare wealth?
Nurmuhammad: Maybe there is some wealth that is not found in any other planet.

Reader: This wealth is where people live.
Princess: Say the answer to this riddle yourself.
Reader: This rare treasure is language.
Together: Language?
Reader: Language is not only a means of communication between people, but also a symbol of the formation and development of the nation. Language is one of the symbols of the state, protected by law.

Feruza: Language is the pride of the people
This is the word of the grandfathers
Mother tongue title
State language status.

(Students sing the song "Uzbek language - my own language" in an accompanying voice.)

SCENE ACTIVITY:

Boy: Well, that's a damn example
made me dizzy
It made my eyes sting
Help me, dad.
Dad: Son, raise your head,
You are not alone with me.
Boy: Excerpt from exercises
They ordered to draw again
Please my dear
You help me.
Mother: Don't worry, my son,
We find this section.
Define a practice
We draw the bottom yes
Son: Grandma, don't sleep
Here's a brush for you.
Draw a picture from a fairy tale
Cat on a chain.
Grandma: No, I'm old, my eyes are dim.
(The child cries)
Grandma: Okay, let's draw a cat.
Boy: Okay, now I'm a little bit
Let's play in the yard.
I'm tired
Let me take a break.
Mehriniso: Wake up cheerfully in the morning,
With a bag on his shoulder
He was in a hurry to go to school.
But sad and sad
He came back from school.
Mother: What did you do, my dear?
Boy: See for yourself.
Dad: No, tell me first.
Son: Dad gave you 5, you got 4 months, grandma gave you 3.
Dad: What about yourself?

Boy: Don't you know, it's hard to study at school.
All: Mothers without you,
If it's not you guys,
It will be boring to read,
If you are not
School will be boring.

"Miracle" planet

A forest scene will be shown on the slide. Pupils dressed as animals take the stage.

Princess: Is this a forest?
Nurmuhammad: No, this is the "Miracle" planet. Animals here can speak human language.
Princess: I don't believe it.
Tiger: Why, don't you believe, all the animals and plants on this planet can be understood in its language.
(Girls dressed as cats dance to "Rain, rain go away")
The stage view is shown: (a monkey sits on the stage with a tablet)

Modern muchal wedding.

The monkey had a big wedding,
At the same time.
Nearby guests,
On the monkey's site.
Lolo from the far north
Yakhmalak posted a picture.
From Jasmin banana,
The monkey's eyes were full.
Mougli also has fruit,
A delicious mango.
Beauty and the Beast-
They gave a tango.
Seeing the emerald chest,
The host is crazy.
A generous, kind farmer -
He wrote "Open Table".
so all day

Friends overflowed.
Well, unfortunately, the tablet,
Out of power.

Princess: Planet of the Wonders is indeed a wonderland.
Nurmuhammad: The weather is also very pleasant.
Asaloy: Because we always follow the golden rules.
Malika, Nurmuhammad: What are the golden rules?

Pupils in the form of animals, flowers and trees appear on the stage:

Rule 1: Protect and preserve natural resources so that these resources will be available to future generations.

Rule 2: Plant and care for trees in schools, yards and streets.

Rule 3: Grow and propagate flowers at home and in classrooms.

Rule 4: Do not throw garbage into ditches and water bodies.

Rule 5: Do not burn fallen leaves of trees in autumn.

Rule 6: Make nests for birds, hang them on trees and feed them.

Princess: Now we follow these golden rules.
Nurmuhammad: We will tell our peers about it.
Host: We have reached the last destination of today's journey. This planet is the planet of "Refinement".

(Students perform sports exercises on stage; a song about wrestlers, boxers, gymnasts and tennis players, athletes is performed.)

Nurmuhammad: What is happening here?
Princess: I think these children must be the stars of this planet.
Nurmuhammad: Go, let's get to know them.
Together: Hello, guys.
Nurmuhammad: We visited from planet Earth.
Princess: Is it true that you all play sports on this planet?
Umid: Yes, after all, sport is a guarantee of health.
Parizoda: How much attention is paid to sports on the

planet where you live?

Nurmuhammad: Seeing once is better than hearing a thousand times. My tablet has great information about it.

(A short video about famous athletes is shown on the screen)

Shohsanam: The youth of a country where sports are paid attention to this level will be healthy.

Princess: Let's go back to our country.

Suhrob: Be our dear guest.

Nurmuhammad: No, homesickness is above all else.

Malika: You're right, I also kept my house a lot.

Nurmuhammad: Goodbye friends, we are glad to meet you.

Malika: When you go to planet Earth, visit beautiful Uzbekistan.

Hamro: We are certainly going to visit Uzbekistan with the intention of getting to know the hospitable young people who are always eager to see the unique country that has created a lot of opportunities for young people.

Nurmuhammad: See you later...

Dinora: Be safe.

(All students go on stage. The song "Uzbekistanim" plays on the screen. Students sing together.)

"UZBEKISTAN - MY FAVORABLE COUNTRY"

The stage is festively decorated, on the walls there are pictures of the prosperity of our country, achievements of the years of independence, and posters with proverbs about the Motherland.

Host: - Hello, distinguished guests, dear teachers, dear students! Today we would like to present to you our event called "Uzbekistan-Jonajon Watanim".

(The national anthem of the Republic of Uzbekistan is played).

Host: - Motherland... the land that brought up so many dear people, was the cradle of great scientists and generals. There is country, there is country. There is a country, there is a people. The Homeland is desolate without you, the Homeland is prosperous without you. That's why in ancient times, those who honored the country were called ``people", and those who lived with the values of the country were called ``patriots".

1st student: - Even spring is not beautiful in a foreign land.

2nd student: - A man is without a country, a nightingale is without a song.

3rd student: - It is not for nothing that it is said to live and serve the Motherland.

Host: - We call our country an independent Motherland. This old country played the strings so that now the image of Uzbekistan is appearing in the eyes of the countries of the world from its magical sounds. Today we honor our perspective, our will, our independence. We sing our holiday in songs and poems.

(The song "Why do I love Uzbekistan?" is played).

Pupils will read the poem "Mother Earth" by Iqbal Mirza.

1st student:- Saints, you are the cradle of geniuses,
You are the door of heaven where the patterns are found.
You are the song of life

You are dear, you are holy, O place of worship,
Uzbekistan, fatherland, motherland!

2nd student:- Your vultures are in my heart,
Which country has great Temurs?
Semurglari, who survived the fires,
You are dear, you are holy, O place of worship,
Uzbekistan, fatherland, motherland!

3rd student: - You became an amulet on someone's chest,
You became dust in someone's eyelash,
Sometimes, March, you were a humor to a boy,
You are dear, you are holy, O place of worship,
Uzbekistan, fatherland, motherland!

4th student: - As a guardian of the legacy of the original child,
The dreams of a free nation are like the sky,
If I say my grandfather's name, it's like an epic
You are dear, you are holy, O place of worship,
Uzbekistan, fatherland, motherland!

5th student: - Those who do not know how to care for their parents-
The two are not one and the same,
Those who cried hard as dirt...
You are dear, you are holy, O place of worship,
Uzbekistan, fatherland, motherland!

6th student: - In the tracks of your rivers, there is a river,
The generation of geniuses are also geniuses!
If he is devoted, he is devoted to this country,
If you are self-sacrificing, be self-sacrificing to this country:
Uzbekistan, fatherland, motherland!

Host: - The independent Republic of Uzbekistan has its own state symbols: anthem, coat of arms, flag and constitution. The state flag of the Republic of Uzbekistan was approved on November 18, 1991 at the special VII session of the Oliy Majlis.

Student 1: - My flag is blue

A sign from the sky.
Always in every color,
Good things are shared.

2nd student: - The blue color reflects nature, the source of life, our clear sky.

Student 3: - The white color on the flag is a symbol of sacred peace. White color means purity, innocence, purity.

4th student: - Green color is a symbol of life and renewal. In many nations, it is a symbol of happiness, hope and joy.

5th student: - The red lines are the rivulets of life force that are beating energetically in our body.

Student 6: - The image of the crescent moon is related to our historical values, eternal traditions, and spiritual strength. The crescent represents the achieved independence, freedom.

Host: - The State Emblem of the Republic of Uzbekistan was approved at the 10th session of the Oliy Majlis on July 2, 1992.

1st student: - On the coat of arms of Uzbekistan
There is a proud humo bird
That's why Uzbek,
Virtue is a constant work.
The eight-pointed star,
It's not night, it's broad daylight,
On one side there are spikes,
On the side of pride-cotton!

Student 2: - On December 8, 1992, the Constitution of the Republic of Uzbekistan was adopted. On December 10, 1992, our country got its national anthem.

Host: - Loving the country means...

Student 1: - Knowing the history of one's people well and being proud of it...

2nd student: - Preserving ancient monuments, old buildings, rich material heritage created by ancestors...

3rd student: - It is understood to be able to appreciate beautiful traditions, customs and customs, and to continue them.

Host: - Everyone loves the country in a different way.

But no matter how we express our love for the country, we must always remember that this dear Motherland belongs to all of us, and we are all responsible for its bright future.

(The event ends with an excerpt from Muhammad Yusuf's poem "Uzbekistan").

Host: - Our shield, if anyone tries to kill you,
May the spirit of Alpomish be with each of your sons.
Let's take care of you, kiss like a flower
The beasts can't get close to your fortress.
ALL: - We will wait for you, Uzbekistan,
We will not give you to anyone, Uzbekistan!

"MATHEMATICS NIGHT"

The scene is decorated with mathematical numbers, examples of various operations.

Host 1: It was played every morning
My great hymn.
Respect every line
Full hymn.

Host 2: The most beautiful song
free glue
my holy hymn,
Full hymn.

(Children in festive clothes enter the stage. They sing a hymn.)

(Children in heraldic clothes enter).

Announcer 1: - E-he-he-eey,
Don't say I didn't hear
Those who love holidays,
Today is a celebration.
Spectators
Time is still a world,
You will be full of joy
You will see a great show

Herald 2: - People are people,
Don't say I didn't hear.
Those who hear, do not smile.
Today in our school
The holiday will be big.
To the morning of mathematics
You should come too.

Leader 2: Thank you, scholars,
Thank you, my children.

Leader 1: Let's entertain our grandparents by telling our poetic riddles and proverbs and playing mathematical games.
answer questions with each other)

NUMEROUS PROVERBS.

Student: - Don't count eight!

Student: - One He who sows a year reaps a hundred years of pearls.

Student: - One forty people ate the raisin

Student: - Cut seven and one!

Student: - Two fifteen to one thirty.

Pupil: - Defeat one with great knowledge , defeat a thousand with great knowledge .

Student: - Oltovlon if he can get it, he will get it

When the tortovlon is finished, he collects the flour.

Student: - One if you plant a vine, One top willow plant.

Student: - Many mouths are one If there is, One mouth will be defeated

Student: - One Say hello to the place where you ate salt for forty days.

Student: - One to a thousand, a thousand to a district .

Student: - Do n't listen to an adult of the little one.

Student: - One a drop of water, an ant saw a river.

Student: - One at home he has no clothes, a bunch of keys on his waist.

Student: - One They don't slaughter cattle on March 3.

Leader 2: - It's time for fun riddles.

Student question: Three pairs of girls, one boy,

They planted flowers from three bushes.

On top of each flower

They poured a bucket of water.

One third of the water

Hides that can be transported.

The boys do the rest.

Where are you, Barno, Safar,

Boy and girl together

How many flowers did he plant?

The most hardworking son

How many buckets of water did he spill?

The student's answer: - He poured 21 buckets of water.

Student's question: We climbed the mountain, 40

children,
> One out of 4 is a girl.
> Each of the sons,
> Pick 10 tulips.
> Girls picked 100 pieces,
> Tell me, my daughter Hilola,
> How many tulips in total?

Student Answer: 400 tulips

Reader's question: 7 kgIs cotton heavy, 7 kg of iron?

Student Answer: Eq

Student 's question : How many times does the number 8 appear in this series of numbers 1, 2, 3 , 4, 5, ...9, 10, 11. , 99?

Student Answer: 20 times

Student's question: Distribute 13 apples to 13 people in such a way that each of them touches one apple and in the basket let one apple remain.

Student's answer: 1 person takes a basket with apples.

Student's question : How many kg does a stork weigh if it stands on one leg 10 kg, and if it stands on two legs ?

Student Answer: 10 kg.

Student's question : how many times should a 6-meter-long piece of wood be sawed by 1 meter ?

Student Answer: 5 times

Reader's question : The big hand of the clock is at 6, what time will it show after 48 seconds?

Student Response: Shows 6 more.

Student's question : You went on vacation from March 24, and returned to school on March 31. How many days were you on vacation?

Student Answer: 31- 23 = 8 days.

Student's question : How many poplar seedlings can be planted on a 21-meter-long piece of land at a distance of 3 meters ?

Student answer: 8

Reader Question : If it's raining at 2 am, can the sun come out 72 hours later?

Student Answer: No, after 72 hours it will be night again.

Student's question: 1 egg cooks in 4 minutes. How many minutes will it take to cook 2 such eggs ?

Student Answer: It takes 4 minutes to cook together.

Student Question: How many Sundays come in a month?

Student Answer: The 4th or 5th Sunday comes.

Student's question: Find the largest three-digit number possible using 3 identical digits .

Student Answer: 999.

Reader's question: 9 flowers were bought on March 9, can these flowers be given equally to two mothers and two daughters?

Student's answer: 3 flowers are given. (Mother, her daughter, granddaughter)

Student's question: The brothers sawed wood. They cut each log into five pieces. It takes 3 minutes to saw each piece . How long did it take to saw two logs ?

Student Answer: 24 minutes.

Student question: Two fathers and two sons ate three eggs for breakfast. Each of them ate one egg. Why is that?

Student's answer: There are 3 of them: grandfather, son, grandson.

Student's question: Is 1 kg1 shilling heavy or half a kg 3 shillings ?

Student Answer: Both are equal

Student's question: Two sheep gators are standing. One's head is facing north and the other is facing south. Can sheep see each other without turning their heads?

Student Answer: They can see because they are each other they are standing .

Student's question: The father is 41 years old, the eldest son is 13 years old, the daughter is 10 years old, the youngest son is 6 years old, after how many years will the father's age be equal to the sum of the ages of all his children ?

Student Answer : $41 + x = 29 + 3x$: $x =$ after 6 years.

Student's question : A pen costs 4 soums more than a pen. 5 pens cost as much as 3 pens. How much does the pen cost?

Student's answer : 10 soums .

Student's question : My brother has 5 pieces of three soms and my sister has 5 pieces of 5 soms. How much money should the sister give to her brother in order for the brother and sister to be equal ?

Student's answer: 1 should give 5 soms.

Student Question: How many Sundays are there at most in a year ?

Student Answer: 53 Sunday.

Student Question: If a person can count 100 grains of wheat in one minute, how long will it take to count 1 billion grains of wheat ?

Student Answer: It takes about 50 years.

Student question: 15 walnuts were placed on the ground. Two players each can take 1, 2, 3 nuts in turn. Whoever has to get the last one nut loses. How many nuts should the starter get for this ?

Student Answer: It should take 2 nuts.

Student Question: The first bag contains 15 blue balls and the second bag contains 12 white balls. A player can get 2 white balls or 3 blue balls at a time . The player who gets the ball wins. How should the starter start the game to win ?

Student Answer : Start by getting two white balls.

Student's question : 6 white and 10 gray socks are mixed in the bag . At least a few socks need to be taken to get at least one pair of the same color socks without looking in the bag .

Student's answer : Three socks are enough.

(Mathematical game will be held as a competition, the winning children will be encouraged.

"FLOWERS AND BIRDS" FESTIVAL

The school stage is decorated with beautiful flowers and birds in a special festive way, soft music is playing. Two presenters appear on the stage.

Leader 1 : (Looking at the flowers) - My friend, look, it's such a beautiful scene. Such beautiful flowers. Aren't these a real miracle of nature?

2nd presenter : - Yes, you are right, flowers are a symbol of true beauty. Today's holiday is also called by the name of this rare miracle of nature - flowers. Look how many guests have gathered for the celebration. Let's say hello to them.

1st presenter : - When you say hello, flowers open
Nightingales walk when you say hello
The sun laughs when you say hello,
The light of goodness shines on the tongues.
2nd starter :
- Hello, dear guests of our circle,
Hello, people of knowledge!
Respected fathers and mothers, hello!
Greetings, children with smiles on their faces!
Student 1: - Peace be in the world,
Let the world be full of flowers!
Children like us
Let him play and laugh in the gardens.
2nd student : - We love holidays,
We have a lot of holidays.
Lover of good souls,
It's always spring in the country.

Leader 1 : - Children, look who came to our circle as a guest. (Bahoroy, wearing flowers in his hair, visits and bows down to greet him).

Pupils : (in unison): - After all, this is Baharoy-ku!
2nd host : - Welcome, Baharoy!
Baharoy: (bowing).
Here I am, beautiful spring,
I have come to you.

I gave life to the trees
Buds, roots.
With my white apricot blossoms,
With my warm sunshine.
Seven rainbows
Green and sometimes on fire,
I came as a guest, guys.

1st host : Spring today, our students want to please you by reciting poems about Navruz, spring holidays and events.

Student 1: When spring comes to my country
The garden became blue.
May the wind blow
Opened smallpox, lola.
The waters flow and rustle,
Lovely voice.
Peaceful
The song of birds.
The swallow croaks,
Smiling from the coal.
The sun comes out
Smiling at us every morning.

Student 2: A bouquet of spring flowers for you
My sincere greetings to you
Live a century and another half a quarter
Friends, have a blessed Navroz.

Student 3: We love holidays,
 We have a lot of holidays
Lover of good souls
It's always spring in the country.

(Song and dance about spring.)

1. Wind : Wind, wind, wind
I am the wind with thick hair.
Clearing the clouds
Reading in all directions
I'm coming to you
I have enough strength!

2. Lightning : Boom-boom, boom-boom,
As if the stones were shining.
Suddenly lightning flashed,
They start falling to the ground.
I know these stones
Not a single one falls.
It's a flower, a flower,
It's dark from Jala.
3. Rain : O humble raindrop,
I like you very much.
Singing joyfully,
Where are you going?
Your blue zilal water,
My land is full of blood.
Therefore, yield
It spreads over my country.
4. Rainbow: Turf-colored rainbow,
Lights after the rain.
Delighting the tongues,
Scattered glitters.

Baharoy : Thank you readers, you have told me wonderful information and stories about me, I am very happy about it. Now I will be with you for three months.

Leader 2 : Thank you for your spring visit.

Leader 1 : - Children, do you know poems about flowers?

Children: - Yes!

1st student: Smallpox.
- You told me about the spring,
It was not easy to wait.
A heart longing for you
My beloved flower, the flower.

2nd student : - I saw you in the park
Velvet hill, in the mountains
In green meadows.
You are a smallpox.
Boycechak, boycechak

My beloved flower, the flower.
3rd student: - Lola, lola lolajon
Your place of work is in the field
Lola, lola lolajon
Did you endure the rain?
Student 4: Chuchmomaman, chuchmoma,
I open for you.
Spreading my fragrance
Open your eyes
(Father the gardener comes in and paints the flowers).

Gardener father : - Do you guys like flowers?
Children: - Yes.
Gardener father : - Give them a picture. how beautiful, how beautiful. Now I want to know your opinion about flowers.

1st student : - Grandfather, where there are flowers, there is beauty, peace, smiles and joy.

Student 2 : It is difficult to imagine beautiful nature without flowers, so we should always protect and multiply them.

3rd student : - If we take care of the flowers in the fields and flower gardens instead of plucking them, isn't this the preservation of true beauty? If we pluck the flowers, they will wither, but how much better it is if they open and delight our eyes. Let us refrain from noticing them.

4th student : - You really need to be kind to flowers, but also to all the green treasures of nature. Hundreds of plant species are currently included in the "Red Book" for the cruelty of humans to nature.

Gardener father : - Good luck, my children! Your deep thoughts made me happy. Flowers like you will turn our country into a beautiful garden in the future. I believe it.

2nd presenter : - Friend, students have a lot of information about flowers.

Leader 1: - Yes, you said it right. Do you know that when spring comes, birds fly to our country from far away. Today, after all, we are celebrating the Feast of Birds.

Speaker 2 : Yes, birds are our friends. Let's ask the children what they know about birds.

Leader 1 : - Children, what do you know about birds?

1st student : - With the arrival of spring, the birds that flew to hot countries return to our country. These include a swallow, a nightingale, and a goldfinch.

2nd student : - Many birds live in one place throughout the year. Such birds include chittak, warbler, blue dove, partridge, sparrow.

Leader 2 : - Do you know poems about birds?

Student 3 : The bells are chirping
Nightingales sing.
Swallows sing.
If all the birds are jam.

Student 4: Deep swallow,
Open your door quickly.
Here is the ear, here is the grain
Your address is this apartment.

Student 5 : Cranes fly a lot.
The swallows are singing.
The horn is in the bosom of the sheep
 White cranes play.

Student 6 : What is the name of this bird?
Water forest
Sing a song
That's why the name is kakku.

Find :

1 . The wings are fluffy, feathery,
Letter carrier and courier.
Even if the mountains and deserts increase
The address is easy to find. (Pigeon)

2 . Long beak, leg
There are no words to describe it.
That is why he is in the water
Sira does not sink. (stork)

3.   Just kidding
There is a lot of skill in it.

That's why the birds
He's doing it. (brain)

SCENE ACTIVITY:

Author : One day, a nightingale was singing in the bosom of flowers, her favorite place, in the meadow. He loves flowers very much and at the same time the flowers loved the nightingale. *(Song)*

Author : At that time, the king of Kashgar was hunting with his loyal servants and fell in love with the sound of the nightingale, and he ordered his servants to carry it away in his golden cage.

King: Friends, nightingale me
His voice burned.
To my sad heart
Joy brought joy.
Put him in a cage
I'm going to my castle
Nice voice
Let's make everyone happy.
(Navkars shake the flowers and carry away the nightingale in a net.)

Shah: Saira, please please me.
Nightingale: What should I sing, my king?
I suffocated in a cage.
I remember what I am
Every minute in breath.
I miss my flowers
I miss my country.
Always happy and cheerful
Every day I sing.
(Song "Missing the Homeland")

Shah : How sad I am,
I didn't think I was bad.
Forgive me, nightingale,

Go to your country.

Nightingale : Thank you my king, thank you.

(The king leaves, the flowers enter the stage, the nightingale enters the garden, and the song is raised, everyone plays. They leave the stage with a bow.)

(Then students give information about birds).

Student 1 : The crow belongs to the sparrow family of the bird class. They live in forests, parks, and riverbanks. In winter, they rarely come to cities and winters.

2nd student : Kyrgyz, the eagle is a member of the family of birds of prey. Kyrgyz is distributed in Europe, Asia and Africa.

Student 3 : Ukki is the biggest among butterflies. Two ear-like balls of feathers stand on top of his head. Ukki feeds mostly on various rodents, sometimes it also catches and eats spiders and some birds.

Student 4 : Ducks originated from wild ducks 3000 years ago. Because duck eggs do not taste very good, they are usually raised for their meat. Mallards can be found in the water bodies of Central Asia.

5th student : Chickens are the most common domestic poultry. Today's chicken breeds are descended from wild bankiv chickens that live in tropical forests.

1st presenter : Dear friends, our evening dedicated to the "Festival of Flowers and Birds" has come to an end. Dear readers, each of us should be kind to nature and preserve the natural beauty of nature.

Leader 2: Protection of nature, rational use of its resources is the sacred duty of every person. Save mother nature, dear readers!

(Students end the night with the song "Save Nature")

Jumanyozova Mukhabbat
Olimboyeva Malohat

ORGANIZING EXTRA-CLASS ACTIVITIES IN PRIMARY CLASSES

(Scenarios of spiritual and educational events)

Editor	B. Botirov
Technical editor	Dilshod Khorozbayev
Designer	Bahadir Tokhliyev
Pager	Bekzod Rakhmatov

www.ingramcontent.com/pod-product-compliance
Lightning Source LLC
LaVergne TN
LVHW010556070526
838199LV00063BA/4985